# The Mountain and
# the Migration

# The Mountain and the Migration

## A GUIDE TO HAWK MOUNTAIN

REVISED AND EXPANDED EDITION

# James J. Brett

Illustrations by
**Frank Fretz**

Raptor identification plates by
**Frederick William Wetzel**

Photographs by
**William R. Fink, Jr., and Joseph Snook**

**Cornell University Press**

Ithaca and London

For Joseph and Helen Taylor

Revised and expanded edition first published 1991 by Cornell University Press. First edition published 1986 by Hawk Mountain Sanctuary Association.

Library of Congress Cataloging-in-Publication Data

Brett, James J.
    The mountain and the migration : a guide to Hawk Mountain / by James J. Brett ; illustrations by Frank Fretz ; raptor identification plates by Frederick William Wetzel ; photographs by William R. Fink, Jr., and Joseph Snook. — Rev. and expanded ed.
        p.  cm.
    Includes bibliographical references and index.
    ISBN 0-8014-9613-6 (pbk. : alk. paper)
    1. Birds of prey—Pennsylvania—Hawk Mountain Sanctuary.  2. Bird watching—Pennsylvania—Hawk Mountain Sanctuary—Guide-books.
3. Hawk Mountain Sanctuary (Pa.)—Guide-books.  I. Title.
QL696.F3B74   1991
598'.07'23474817—dc20                                              91-14929

Printed in the United States of America

♾ The paper in this book meets the
minimum requirements of the American National
Standard for Information Sciences—Permanence of Paper
for Printed Library Materials, ANSI Z39.48-1984.

# Contents

The folding insert inside the back cover contains a map of the Hawk Mountain Sanctuary trails, drawings of the migrant raptors in flight, and a guide to the panorama from the North Lookout.

# Foreword

No one knows how long the hawks have been using the ridge of Blue Mountain during their annual passage southward, but certainly for thousands of years, back to the time of the last ice sheet. Audubon, who lived within a day's horseback ride, did not know of Hawk Mountain. Certainly as far back as 100 years ago some Pennsylvania gunners knew of the flights; they initiated the slaughter, but the birders stopped it.

I first became aware of the annual tragedy at Hawk Mountain in 1925 when I read an article in the *Wilson Bulletin* by my fellow bird artist George Sutton, who was at that time with the Pennsylvania Game Commission. He had gathered up 158 hawks, all killed by a few gunners "in a remarkably short time." Science was served by the article, but no judgment was passed on the slaughter. Remember, we were still in the specimen-tray era of ornithology.

But in 1932 Henry Collins and Richard Pough opened people's eyes. In *Bird Lore*, the predecessor of *Audubon Magazine*, Pough wrote:

On top of Blue Mountain, above Drehersville, Schuylkill County, an appalling slaughter was going on.... When 100 or 150 men armed with pump guns, automatics, double-barreled shotguns, are sitting on top of the mountain looking for a target . . . no bird is safe. . . . Wounded hawks were strung up in trees as decoys. Blinded pigeons were tied to a long pole; when a hawk came over, the pole was waved so that the pigeon would flutter wildly.

The slaughter was rationalized by the gunners; they were "getting rid of the killers." The Pennsylvania Game Commission provided incentive by offering a five-dollar bounty on goshawks.

Few conservationists had noticed Sutton's article in the *Wilson Bulletin*, but hundreds became indignant when they read the one in *Bird Lore*, among them an indomitable woman, Rosalie Barrow Edge. It was because of her that we have Hawk Mountain Sanctuary as we know it today.

I first met Rosalie Edge when I was a teenager in New York, attending art school. During the month of May I sometimes saw her with her binoculars in Central Park, where to this day

Manhattan birders go in the morning to see the migrant warblers. I was even invited to a couple of the secret meetings chaired by Williard Van Name in her apartment, where they planned their attacks on T. Gilbert Pearson, president of the Audubon Society, prior to the society's annual members' meeting. She was particularly irked by Pearson's seeming lack of concern for birds of prey. As a naive young man from the boondocks of upstate New York, I sat with open mouth at these clandestine meetings, not fully aware of what the plotting was about.

Because of the pressure, Pearson sent Robert Porter Allen, a new staff member, to check on things at Hawk Mountain. Arriving too late in the season and finding no favorable winds, however, he encountered few hawks and almost no gunners. His report was anything but alarmist, and the Audubon Society did nothing. Rosalie Edge decided to take action herself.

In late summer of 1933, Rosalie Edge traveled from New York City to Hawk Mountain with six hundred dollars to secure an option to purchase the property. She signed an agreement with the owner of a tombstone company and the hotel that would later be known as Schaumboch's Tavern to purchase some fourteen hundred acres for thirty-five hundred dollars. She had until December 1935 to raise the balance.

The option secure, Rosalie Edge returned to New York. It wasn't until the following year that she met a young ornithologist on Cape Cod whom she felt could be the first warden at Hawk Mountain, beginning in September 1934. It was because of this young man and his new bride, Irma, who dedicated half their lives to the mountain, that Hawk Mountain Sanctuary became a viable reality.

Maurice Broun became hooked on birds at the age of thirteen when he walked into the Boston Public Garden to get away from the confusion of the city. There he discovered a delightful group of people, all straining their necks to look up into the treetops. He strained his neck, too, and a kind woman offered him a pair of field glasses, through which he saw a magnolia warbler—the most wonderful thing he had ever seen. Even the name fell like music on his ears. I first met Maurice on Cape Cod, late in the summer of 1931 or 1932, when he was banding birds at the Austin Research Station. When we renewed our acquaintance several years later, he had married Irma, a Cape Cod woman, and they had just been asked by Mrs.

Edge to start work at Hawk Mountain. It would become their life's work.

The beginnings of the sanctuary and Maurice and Irma's part in those beginnings are recorded in *Hawks Aloft*, written by Maurice, and also in *The View from Hawk Mountain* by Michael Harwood. This new book by Jim Brett, curator of the sanctuary, brings us up to date on Hawk Mountain Sanctuary.

In those early years, the Brouns were guarding the mountain and lived in a little stone house beside the road, a dwelling with a sinister history. I thought about the ghost of Schaumboch when I crawled into my sleeping bag on a cot under the back porch. The strange noises I heard at night in the stonework behind me proved to be a woodrat—known to the Brouns as "old cleft ear"—who was sitting at the foot of my cot when I awoke.

I was elected to Hawk Mountain's board of directors in 1948, along with its future president, Joe Taylor. In those days there was no problem finding a boulder to sit on at the North Lookout. And it was always a joy to watch the aerial parade if the wind was in the northwest. Plenty of redtails and sharpshins, a few Cooper's, perhaps a goshawk or a peregrine, and, best of all, the occasional eagle. A Sunday visitor only a few years earlier would have found a veritable army of men with pump guns and automatic shotguns blasting away at anything that flew by.

Many of the flowers in the *Field Guide to Wildflowers*, which I wrote with Margaret McKenny, were drawn at Hawk Mountain. And it was on this mountain that my *Field Guide to the Birds of Britain and Europe* was conceived. In the fall of 1949 Maurice Broun introduced me at the gate to Guy Mountfort, a visitor from England. Mountfort said there really should be a field guide for Europe patterned after my American guide. As we walked up the trail we discussed things further, and before we reached the North Lookout we had wrapped things up. The book was eventually published in fourteen languages.

Over the years the number of human visitors to Hawk Mountain has been staggering. We are at the point where they outnumber the hawks most days, such as on the October weekend when we celebrated the sanctuary's golden anniversary. Ten thousand people swarmed over the mountaintop, but because the wind was from the southeast we saw few birds other than the local turkey vultures, soaring lazily on the thermals.

During the thirty-two years that Maurice and Irma reigned

as king and queen of the mountain they not only guarded the lookout but also monitored the flights and guided the hordes of visitors. Upon their retirement, Al Nagy became curator and carried on the tradition for another fifteen years.

Hawk Mountain directly saved thousands of birds of prey from sudden destruction, but its influence on hawk protection has reached beyond Pennsylvania, and indeed beyond North America. It has entered the new fields of education and raptor research. Never have I met a more enthusiastic staff, not to mention the helpful young interns and corps of volunteers who make things run smoothly.

Hawk Mountain Sanctuary has come of age. I love the place!

ROGER TORY PETERSON

# Preface

*The Mountain and the Migration* is a guide to Hawk Mountain Sanctuary, one of the world's prime hawk-watching locations. Treating a broad range of subject matter within a narrow geographical focus, the guide provides the reader with the information necessary to get the most out of a visit to the sanctuary. It can also be used as a general natural history guide to the larger Appalachian region in Pennsylvania, New Jersey, and southern New York.

Hawk Mountain Sanctuary, located along the Kittatinny Ridge of the Appalachian Mountain system, is unique, and to know it well would require years of field study and a large library of natural history texts. A few people have made the sanctuary and the surrounding countryside the subject of close study for years. The chapters in this guide draw on the accumulated knowledge of those who have been closely associated with the mountain and with the cultural and natural history that make it a very special place.

The guide describes the cultural background of Hawk Mountain, summarizes the complex geological processes that formed it, discusses the indigenous plants and animals, and treats in depth the yearly autumn migration of tens of thousands of birds of prey, that singular event for which Hawk Mountain Sanctuary is best known by naturalists throughout the world.

Two chapters, more than half the book, are devoted to the dynamics of raptor migration and the identification of the birds of prey that migrate past the sanctuary each autumn. They offer, I believe, the most complete treatment of northeastern migrant raptors currently available. Drawing on and synthesizing the knowledge of observers with thousands of hours of field experience, the field descriptions provide solid techniques for the identification of raptors in flight. Fred Wetzel, a former member of the Hawk Mountain staff and a superb artist, drew the illustrations of the birds of prey—the most varied and accurate flight portraits of these raptors ever published. The plates can be used on any ridgetop observation point from Nova Scotia and the Great Lakes to the southern Appalachians and Texas. They can also be used to identify raptors during their autumn and spring migrations along the East Coast.

The intent of any work dealing with field natural history is to spur the reader to go farther in the quest to know the natural world. I hope *The Mountain and the Migration* will do just that.

The preparation of this guide began, I suspect, on my first visit to the North Lookout nearly forty years ago. I have added impressions over the years, first as a youngster, then during high school and college, later as a teacher taking students on field trips, and for the last twenty years as a member of Hawk Mountain's staff. When it came time to put those impressions into words, I called upon some of the people who have taught me so much along the way.

Peggy Judd and her late husband, Archibald Judd, longtime Hawk Mountaineers, provided me with insights into the flora of this section of the Appalachians. Matthew Spence and Hans Wilkins, deans of our local botanists, carefully reviewed the plant checklist. The five of us shared secrets about locations of rare orchids and ferns and ancient oaks.

My longtime friends and colleagues Judy Wink and Joe Lankalis, both students of Maurice Broun's and superb naturalists, fielded my questions about many aspects of the natural history of the area. I have been an eager and willing student of theirs over the years.

Tom Wright of the National Science Foundation and Craig Kochel of Bucknell University, both geologists who specialize in the Appalachian region, helped me understand the complicated geological processes that shaped the sanctuary's topography.

A whole corps of hawk-watchers and counters reviewed the identification plates and species descriptions; Laurie Goodrich and Jim Olmes, especially, worked through draft after draft until this guide went to press.

The Maurice Broun Library, located in the Department of Biology at Muhlenberg College, gave me permission to quote from Maurice Broun's unpublished diary in chapter 1.

The many friends who have spent countless hours with me on the North Lookout and who have served as sounding boards for my ideas about natural history and bird-of-prey identification know who they are, and while I cannot list them here, they have my appreciation. Finally, my students in the field courses and workshops taught on the mountain for two decades have stimulated my pursuit of the natural and cultural history of these hills, and I thank them. Hawk Mountain Sanctuary is truly a school in the clouds. *The Mountain and the Migration* is dedicated to that concept.

JIM BRETT

*Hawk Mountain Sanctuary, Kempton, Pennsylvania*

# The Mountain and
# the Migration

# CHAPTER 1

# Once upon a Mountain

Hawk Mountain Sanctuary is situated on the border of Berks and Schuylkill counties in eastern Pennsylvania. The name Hawk Mountain undoubtedly derives from the yearly passage of hawks along the Kittatinny Ridge, the local name of this part of the Appalachian Mountains. The Appalachians in Pennsylvania form what geologists call the Ridge and Valley Province and comprise, in the northeastern part of the state, a series of parallel ridges that run from northeast to southwest. The southernmost ridge, where Hawk Mountain Sanctuary is located, is called the Kittatinny.

Early written accounts refer to the areas north of Philadelphia and west of Allentown only as the frontier west of the Delaware River or the wilderness north of Reading. For early local history one must rely on stories passed down from generation to generation. Many of these tales concern events that occurred at the old hotel along the Mountain Road. On the east side of Hawk Mountain, a short distance from the Visitor Center, is Schaumboch's Tavern, a small cottage that was the focal point of the mountain's history long before it became a sanctuary.

Tracing the lineage of the cottage's ownership has proven difficult, largely because the first census-takers who traveled Penn's Woods trying to establish tax rosters missed its remote location. As far as is known, the cottage, of sandstone and chestnut, was built about the time of the American Revolution by one Jacob Gerhardt.

Gerhardt, as a young boy, lived in Eckville, a small hamlet two miles east of the cottage. His father (also named Jacob), mother, grandmother, and six brothers and sisters met untimely deaths at the hands of Lenape Indians in 1755. Young Jacob was the sole survivor of that massacre in Eckville.

D. A. Brunner's classic, *The Indians of Berks County, Pennsylvania, being a summary of all the Tangible Records Of The Aborigines Of Berks County*, relates the horror in grisly detail. Quoted is a letter written on February 15, 1755, by Valentine Probst to Jacob Levan:

Mr. Levan:—I cannot omit writing about the dreadful circumstances in our township, Albany. The Indians came yesterday about eight

1

o'clock to Frederick Reichelderfer's house, as he was feeding his horses, and two of the Indians ran upon him, and followed him into a field ten or twelve perches off; but he escaped and ran toward Jacob Gerhardt's house, with a design to fetch some arms. When he came near Gerhardt's he heard a lamentable cry, "Lord Jesus! Lord Jesus!"—which made him run back toward his own house; but before he got quite home, he saw his house and stable in flames; and heard cattle bellowing and thereupon ran away again.

Two of his children were shot; one of them was found dead in the field, the other was found alive and brought to Hackenbrook's house, but died three hours after. All his grain and cattle were burned up. At Jacob Gerhardt's they killed one man, two women, and six children. Two children slipped under the bed; one of which was burned; the other escaped and ran a mile to get to the people. We desire help or we must leave our homes.

Yours,<br>Valentine Probst

Brunner's work details Indian atrocities committed against the settlers, but it fails to give the reasons behind the attacks.

Hawk Mountain Sanctuary lies on the crest of the ridge the Delaware Indians called Keekachtatenin—later corrupted to Kittatinny—the "endless mountain." The Delaware considered it their most sacred mountain. Chiefs were drawn to the prominences now known as the North Lookout and the Pinnacle to worship Manito, the Great Spirit.

The Delaware Indians who inhabited the Hawk Mountain area were members of the Unami, or Turtle Clan, and referred to themselves as Lenape ("original people"). In the mid-seventeenth century about eleven thousand members of the Delaware Nation lived north to Long Island and south and west to Delaware Bay and the Susquehanna River. (The first humans inhabited this area during the period 10,500 to 6,000 B.C. and accompanied the retreating glacial sheet. These dates have been established by carbon dating of human remains.) A major settlement of the Unami was located about twelve miles southeast of Hawk Mountain, near the present town of Virginville,

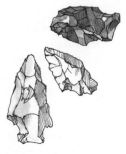

and small bands of Indians lived and hunted on either side of the mountain. Even today artifacts can be found in fields along Pine Creek to the east and the Little Schuylkill River to the west. The Delaware lived peacefully with the British colonists for most of the eighteenth century. Periodically cheated and lied to by both the British and French, however, they felt compelled to retaliate. For the most part their lands had been purchased for outrageously small sums or traded for goods of little value, and they were being forced farther and farther from their homelands. Anticipating Indian uprisings, the British erected small forts along the Kittatinny Ridge between the Delaware and Schuylkill rivers for the protection of settlers. Forts were constructed about every twelve miles, but the settlers around isolated Eckville lacked the security of a fort.

On that fateful night in February of 1755 there was one survivor—twelve-year-old Jacob Gerhardt. Why, not many years later, he would decide to build a cottage high on the mountain, even more remote from his native Eckville, remains a mystery. Jacob Gerhardt apparently lived only a short time in the mountainside cottage, for the story goes that he died of tuberculosis at an early age. The last of the Delaware were pushed south and west in the early 1800s, and quiet days returned to Eckville.

During the long period between the Revolutionary and Civil wars, several important furnaces operated on the flanks of the mountain, producing steel shot for firearms. To fuel these furnaces, charcoalmen produced vast amounts of charcoal in the surrounding forest. Remnants of this early industry are still in evidence on the sanctuary. Along old logging roads on both sides of the mountain are charcoal flats, areas where pieces of oak were slowly burned in log enclosures covered with forest duff to prevent air from entering. The ground was sterilized over the years, so that only grasses grow there now, and even those grasses have appeared only recently.

New settlers, mostly of German extraction, were employed as charcoalmen and lumbermen, or they were farmers. They were known as the Pennsylvania Dutch, even though they had come from the Palatinate region of Germany. Many of the names of these families can still be seen on mailboxes along the roads leading to the sanctuary.

In the early 1800s anthracite coal was discovered north of the Kittatinny Ridge. Soon coal supplanted charcoal as the major industrial fuel, and the charcoal industry died out. The population increased to the north as mining towns mushroomed. Names such as Mahanoy City, Shenandoah, and Minersville appeared on early maps. People of Polish, Irish, Welsh, and

Italian ancestry arrived in large numbers to mine the "black diamond." Towns flourished and the inhabitants, for the moment, prospered.

The narrow trail leading from Eckville to Drehersville on the Little Schuylkill River soon bore the deep ruts of horse-drawn wagons. Known as the Mountain Road, it became a main artery connecting the agricultural areas to the east with the coal-mining towns in the north. Wagons laden with produce and household goods made weekly trips to markets in the north. The road over the mountain was long and steep; horses tired quickly in the heat of summer and early autumn. The wayside Gerhardt cottage, inhabited on and off for a quarter of a century, became an important stop for wagon masters and their teams. It was probably during this period that the cottage became known as the Mountain Hotel. While the horses were refreshed at the spring across from the hotel, the teamsters refreshed themselves inside.

About 1850 Matthias Schambacher appeared on the scene and established himself as one in a long line of tavern keepers at the hotel. He would come to be known as "Schaumboch"— the murderous proprietor of an infamous establishment. Stories of horror trickled down the mountain, spreading far and

Schaumboch's Tavern, circa 1875

wide, and citizens of the local communities discussed tales of merchants last seen heading toward Schaumboch's Tavern.

During Schambacher's reign of terror he is reputed to have murdered more than two dozen men. Legend has it that he would get a victim drunk on homemade applejack, lead him from the hotel to the barn, sink an axe into his skull, dump the body in an old hand-dug well, then take the victim's horses and loaded wagon to Port Clinton on the Schuylkill River Canal, where his brother-in-law was lock tender. There the loot would be loaded onto a canal boat and transported to Philadelphia, where it was sold.

Matthias Schambacher died on March 10, 1879, much to the relief of the local citizenry and, it is said, of his wife, Becky, as well. He was laid to rest in the New Bethel Church cemetery, six miles east of the sanctuary. The cemetery's caretaker claimed that during an early summer thunderstorm several months after Schambacher's burial, lightning struck deep into the miscreant's grave. Local people still say that his ghost roams the mountain and that on misty evenings his presence is strongly felt in and around the Mountain Hotel.

While there are no known Schambacher descendents in the area, grandchildren of William Turner, who followed Schambacher as keeper of the tavern, live on both sides of the sanctuary. William Turner made the hotel his home for some twenty years and fathered ten children. His large family, along with the

An early sandstone quarrying operation existed on Hawk Mountain on and off from the late 1800s until about 1920. A few remnants of that operation can still be seen.

The foundation of the brake drum that controlled the descent of the ore cars to the river

Joseph Snook

The breaker at the base of the Slide

Joseph Snook

The Slide, a long-abandoned gravity railroad bed

Joseph Snook

The foundation of the breaker house along the Little Schuylkill River

W. R. Fink, Jr.

comings and goings of the tavern trade, made for lively times in the small two-room cottage of Jacob Gerhardt.

The hotel reached its heyday at the end of the nineteenth century. The increase in the number of farm markets in Orwigsburg, Schuylkill Haven, and Pottsville meant more traffic over the mountain. At the same time there was a small sandstone quarrying operation on top of the mountain. Stone removed from an exposed outcrop was transported by mule-drawn ore cars to a gravity railroad siding track on the edge of the ridge, a location known today as "the Slide" (see illustrations on pages 6 and 7). Here, loaded into larger cars, the stone was eased down the thousand feet to the river by cable. While the loaded car descended, an empty one was hoisted up on the same track at the other end of the cable. Midway along the route was a switch-out, a detour in the track that allowed the descending and ascending cars to pass each other. A small stone breaker along the railroad next to the river crushed the stone; it was then transported by rail to glass manufacturing plants south of the ridge. The quarry was in full swing at the turn of the century but ended shortly thereafter when purer deposits of sandstone were located farther west. Remains of that industry can still be seen along the Slide.

The tavern business on the mountain boomed until Prohibition. By then the Turners had left, and the hotel was occupied on and off by bands of bootleggers, who produced a variety of gin in the cellar. According to Maurice Broun, the sanctuary's first curator, the moonshining took place in the hotel, and the bootleggers lived in a chicken shed in the old orchard. Broun reports in *Hawks Aloft* that it took almost "an entire season to clean up the broken beer and whiskey bottles, the heaps of clam shells and other debris."

After coal replaced charcoal in the furnaces, residents on either side of the Kittatinny Ridge turned to cutting chestnut

and oak for lumber. In the 1920s the chestnut blight obliterated most of the chestnut stands, but lumberjacks continued to cut red oak to supply timbers for the deep-shaft anthracite mines. At the same time local residents intermittently burned the ridgetop to enhance the annual crop of blueberries, a favorite food.

Despite the continual alteration of the slopes and ridges, one thing remained the same: the autumn movement of raptors down the ridges of the Appalachian Mountains. No one knows for sure when the first hawk shooters appeared on Hawk Mountain, but once again, under various owners, Schaumboch's Tavern flourished as gunners stopped by to purchase jugs of moonshine. On weekends shotgun shells were sold along the road. Following a weekend of heavy shooting, local scrap dealers shoveled the spent brass cartridges into burlap bags.

On windy days gunners came armed with shotguns (each person often carried two guns: with constant firing a gun would become too hot to handle) as well as moonshine, anticipation, and an eagerness to destroy any hawk that passed the gunsights. Probably most of the hawk shooters shared the common misconception that raptors were wanton killers, believing that by shooting them they performed a valuable service to the local wildlife. More than that, the shooting was fun and exciting, and provided target practice for the small-game hunting season in late fall. Indeed, when the first of November arrived, the ridges were little visited, as the gunners turned to small game in the farmlands below.

The Pennsylvania Game Commission encouraged hawk shooting by offering bounties on goshawks. Beginning in 1929 hunters were paid five dollars for each goshawk shot between November 1 and May 1. Although the bounty applied only to goshawks, few shooters could (or bothered to) identify birds of prey on the wing but rather gunned down any raptor that flew by. Local game wardens assigned to monitor the shooting and halt the killing of protected species mostly looked the other way.

During this period of fire and brimstone, and far removed from the ridgetop battleground, another campaign was taking root. Wildlife and wild lands were being perceived in new ways by such people as Theodore Roosevelt, John Muir, Gifford Pinchot, and Aldo Leopold. They were reshaping age-old concepts about land use, conservation, and wildlife management at a time when the major conservation organizations were clearly failing in their roles as protectors of North American wildlife.

Richard Pough and Henry Collins examine the slaughtering grounds at the Slide, circa 1932

Richard Pough

During the late 1920s and early 1930s, the burgeoning hawk shooting along Pennsylvania's ridges began to receive widespread attention. A young amateur ornithologist from Philadelphia was one of the first outsiders to discover the shooting grounds at what had come to be known as Hawk Mountain. His name was Richard Pough. On an autumn weekend in 1932, he came to the mountain and stumbled upon one of the most grisly hawk-shooting sites in the east. Pough, his brother, and Henry Collins gathered the dead hawks and lined them up in row upon row. Pough then photographed them. Although he was subsequently unable to convince officials of the National Association of Audubon Societies of the need for hawk protection, his photographs and lectures would nonetheless be instrumental in the campaign to end the slaughter.

Rosalie Barrow Edge heard Richard Pough's appeal at a meeting of the Hawk and Owl Society in New York in 1933 and was deeply distressed at the lack of concern for raptors. Under the banner of the Emergency Conservation Committee, an organization she had started to spread the word about the plight of North American wildlife and wild lands, she began to raise money to purchase Hawk Mountain. Those were difficult times, just after the worst years of the Great Depression; it was hard enough to raise money for "practical" matters, to say nothing of soliciting donations to save wildlife. But Rosalie

Rosalie Barrow Edge, 1948

Maurice and Irma Broun, 1948

Edge was a determined woman as well as one of the most effective champions of conservation this country has produced.

Rosalie Edge founded Hawk Mountain Sanctuary in September of 1933, when she purchased from the owner of a local tombstone company a lease and option to buy 1,393 acres of mountaintop and flank forest land. The option cost $600, which she borrowed from a friend in New York City. Not until December of 1935 was $3,500 raised to fulfill the terms of sale. At a cost of $2.50 an acre Hawk Mountain became the first sanctuary in the world created to protect birds of prey.

Rosalie Edge moved to establish a presence on the mountain even before the land could be purchased, engaging as caretaker for the fall of 1934 a young New England ornithologist named Maurice Broun. Broun and his bride, Irma, could not have imagined what lay in store for them as they traveled south from peaceful Cape Cod. An early diary entry by Maurice Broun, dated Monday, September 10, 1934, reads:

Murky, foggy, dusty, gloomy country, and god-awful nightmare roads all the way—it seemed—to Drehersville, which we reached after four

Maurice Broun sighting a hawk over no. 1, 1950s

hours of driving today. Arriving in the vicinity of Drehersville, we were captivated by the beauty of the hills, the rich meadows and farmland, as well as the quaint charm of the natives, all of whom had a very pleasing smile with which to greet us. It was not long before we found ourselves on the famous Hawk Mountain. Near the scene of the greatest annual slaughter, after having successfully negotiated a two-mile stretch of awful, rocky back road, during which there were no houses whatever, we finally came to the old Turner "hotel" and there made friends with a kindly Dutch woman, and her two small children, who were living in the old dwelling temporarily, it being a sort of summer camp and gunner's rendezvous. After some time we decided to put up here. We were disheartened by the drab and dark interior of the upper quarters; the woman could not make a price until the arrival of her husband Wednesday evening. After dinner Irma and I off to Schuylkill Haven and environs, making divers contacts with which to begin work on the morrow. . . . Got a great deal of information about the mountain and the slaughter . . . and know I'm in for one of the toughest jobs of my life, but 'twill be a rare and very worthwhile experience.

A "rare" and "worthwhile" tenure it proved to be. The Brouns devoted the better part of their lives to the mission Rosalie Edge had set, and carved out of a ridgetop shooting gallery a sanctuary of distinction.

Mostly it was a seat-of-the-pants operation. At first the Brouns were seasonal workers at Hawk Mountain, receiving bare-bones pay plus room and board. They lived with the Henry Koch family in Drehersville, two miles to the west. To work under these conditions was their choice; they believed in Rosalie Edge and her mountain, and they agreed that all monies raised should be used to develop educational programs at the sanctuary and later to promote legislation that would protect the passage of birds of prey. Except for 1943–1945, when Maurice was in the service, the Brouns remained on the job until their retirement in 1966. Their influence and the influence of the sanctuary helped enact laws, state by state, to protect raptors. At last the protection of migrant raptors was made part of the Migratory Bird Treaty Act of 1972, which implements the treaties between the United States, Canada, and Mexico and gives federal protection to all raptors.

Joseph Snook

Located near the Visitor Center, *Spirit of the Heart*, a sculpture of an eagle by artist Mary Taylor, commemorates the work of the founders of Hawk Mountain Sanctuary

Rosalie Edge served as president of the Hawk Mountain Sanctuary Association from the time it was chartered in 1938 until 1962. She raised the money to develop and operate the sanctuary mainly by building a large membership of grass-roots conservationists, most of whom contributed modest sums of money each year. She died in 1962 at the age of eighty-five, but her driving spirit continues to motivate the sanctuary today.

Hawk Mountain Sanctuary quickly became a leader in the field of wildlife conservation. Its educational programs have stimulated widespread interest in birds, in conservation, in the natural history of the Appalachian Mountain, and in careers in the natural sciences. Its annual counts (see appendix 2) and research on birds of prey around the world, and its efforts to protect raptors from shooters, pesticides, and other threats, have achieved lasting results.

Today the association has the support of nearly eight thousand members in the United States and abroad, and Hawk Mountain is visited by about fifty thousand people annually. The association seeks to continue as a leader in the field of wildlife conservation, education, and research while maintaining the sanctuary as a natural area, not only for the enjoyment and education of birders and naturalists but for all visitors.

# CHAPTER 2

# The Lay of the Land

In the brief span of time encompassing human existence, more than a million people have climbed the bold promontory known as the North Lookout of Hawk Mountain Sanctuary and have been inspired by the sweeping panoramas to the west, north, and east. Rising abruptly from the banks of the Little Schuylkill River, the steep ridge culminates in a tumble of sandstone blocks 1,521 feet above sea level. The scene is one of the most impressive in eastern North America. The North Lookout is situated on the front range of the Appalachian Mountains, a ridge known locally as Kittatinny. From the North Lookout the view to the west and north is one of low, undulating ridges and shallow valleys. The northernmost ridge, Broad Mountain, is some twenty-five air miles from the North Lookout. Clearly visible is a man-made gap created during the construction of Interstate Highway 81. Geologists refer to this section of Pennsylvania as the Ridge and Valley Province (see illustration on next page). It is bounded on the north by the Pocono Plateau, on the east by the Great Valley, and on the west by the Allegheny Plateau. East of the Great Valley are the Piedmont, the Coastal Plain, and finally the Atlantic Ocean. To the south, the Great Valley is flanked, in Reading, Pennsylvania, by South Mountain, composed of some of the oldest igneous rock on the North American continent, dating back more than a billion years to the Precambrian era.

The geologic history of the Hawk Mountain region is fascinating. At times covered by great oceans, the area has also witnessed the building and erosion of towering mountains. The Appalachians, of which Hawk Mountain is a part, are the result of a series of movements in the earth's crust that began about 500 million years ago and lasted nearly 300 million years. These mountains were once as grand as the Alps, with peaks soaring some twenty thousand feet above sea level. The Sierras, the Rockies, and the Alps are all much younger, less eroded mountain systems than the Appalachians.

Geologists face a formidable task in attempting to understand the birth and development of landforms. The "layer cake" configuration of, for example, the Grand Canyon of the Colorado River is relatively easy to interpret; one works down

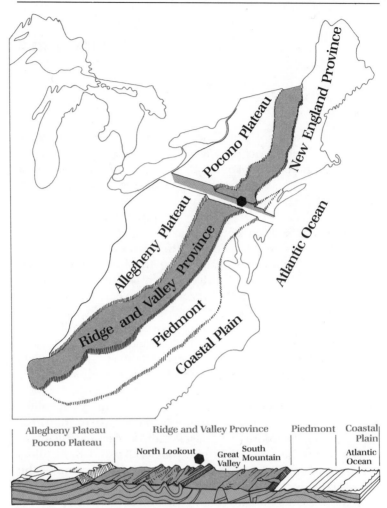

through successively older material. Mountains are different. The titanic forces that shaped mountains folded or fractured and shifted layers of deposited materials so that sometimes the oldest rocks are found on mountaintops, while the valleys hold the youngest ones.

Typically, rocks resistant to erosion stand higher than those that weather easily, the latter being sculpted into adjacent valleys. The rocks on the North and South lookouts, along the Escarpment Trail, and in fact all along the top of the Kittatinny Ridge are Tuscarora sandstone. The Tuscarora, a well-cemented sandstone, is sedimentary rock composed of particles ranging in size from sand grains to large pebbles.

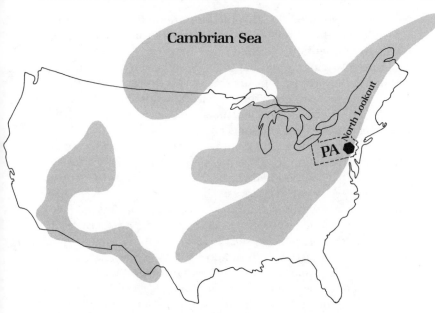

Cambrian Sea

North Lookout

PA

Sediments are carried from higher to lower elevations by three erosional agents—wind, ice, and water—and from lower to higher elevations by tremendous uplifting forces within the earth.

### Birth of the Mountain

The story begins some 500 million years ago in the Cambrian period. At that time Pennsylvania was covered by a shallow tropical sea. Over the next 60 million years the sea floor sank to form a deep trough. A blanket of muddy sediment thousands of feet thick accumulated in the abyss. Pressure and heat from the accumulation of mud transformed the ooze into shale. Later, tectonic movements exerted additional pressure, converting the shale into slate and folding and uplifting the former sea-bottom sediments. Geologists call these deformed slates and shales the Martinsburg Formation, which can be observed in the sanctuary's Aspen Cut campground (see folding map). The uplifted Martinsburg materials formed part of a high mountain range created during the Taconic Orogeny, a 50-million-year period of mountain building.

Erosion cut into these mountains during the next 20 million years, ultimately stripping away part of the folded Martinsburg slates and shales. Finally, during the Silurian period 430 million years ago, erosion gave way to deposition of a new layer of sediments over the beveled layers of slates. Huge Silurian river systems rushed off the Taconic mountains toward the north-west, depositing their sands and gravels in large alluvial fans and river channels. Braided rivers coursed through this alluvium, bringing large quantities of sediment to form deltas and beaches. These deposits are recorded in the Silurian Tuscarora Formation. Thus the Tuscarora sandstones atop North and South lookouts contain the sand grains and gravels that once occupied river channels and beaches.

Fifteen million years later the beach had migrated to the middle of the state. The Taconic mountains had become Taconic hills. Deposition in the valleys was slow. Massive deposits of coarse sediment were covered by muds whose iron oxidized upon contact with the Silurian atmosphere, turning them red. Geologists named the red rocks originating adjacent to the shores of the late Silurian sea the Bloomsburg Formation, after a town north of Hawk Mountain. In this formation are remnants of fishes that lived 400 million years ago. The farmlands immediately north of Hawk Mountain have a reddish hue, the soils having been derived from the Bloomsburg beds of alluvial red rock. In contrast, the farm soils east of North Lookout are tan or brown, having taken their color from the Martinsburg slates and shales.

The shoreline continued to advance and retreat as the ocean level fluctuated throughout the late Silurian and the Devonian. By the beginning of the Devonian, some 400 million years ago, the continental sea was retreating to the west. The accumulation of plant and animal remains in the Devonian sea, a shallow body of water teeming with life, was remarkable. Today just north of the Kittatinny near the town of Deer Lake and east of the town of New Ringgold are quarries whose rocks abound in Devonian fossils—corals, clams, trilobites, snails, crinoids, and sponges—evidence of the proliferation of life in the Devonian sea.

**Westward retreat of shoreline during the Devonian**

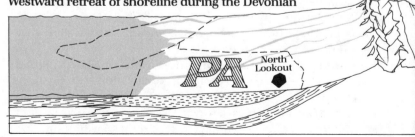

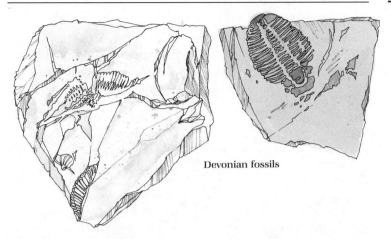

Devonian fossils

Several periods of tectonic movements during the mid to late Paleozoic era produced impressive mountains in the area south and east of Hawk Mountain. Erosion wore away the rocks. The result was the gradual removal of vast quantities of sediment. This sediment was deposited into enormous deltas as rivers dumped their load. Much of this sediment moved west of what is now the sanctuary, giving rise to a steaming, impenetrable jungle of giant horsetails and ferns. In these great deltaic swamps to the north and west soft-tissued trees grew to heights of a hundred feet and enormous dragonflies with two-foot wingspans alighted on the stumps of decaying trees. Splendid fossil beds containing plants of the ancient swamp are found near the town of St. Clair, twenty miles northwest of the sanctuary.

Pennsylvania's famous coal fields originated in these swamps. Coal forms when buried vegetation is subjected to great heat and sediment pressure; the greater the heat and stress, the harder the coal.

Near the end of the Paleozoic era, a final cataclysmic mountain-building event, the Alleghenian Orogeny, occurred. This last squeeze drastically altered all sediments and rocks in the Hawk Mountain area. Mountains were again thrust into the sky. So intense was the tectonic activity that layers of shale and sandstone and fossilized organic sediments were pushed far from the point of deposition. And not only were they shoved, they were folded, tilted, and overturned. This orogeny was responsible for the intense folding visible in the local ridges today.

By the end of the Paleozoic era, 225 million years ago, the great thicknesses of sediment gathered in Silurian and Devonian oceans had been vaulted to the sky for the last time, and

## Geologic map and cross section
## of Hawk Mountain vicinity

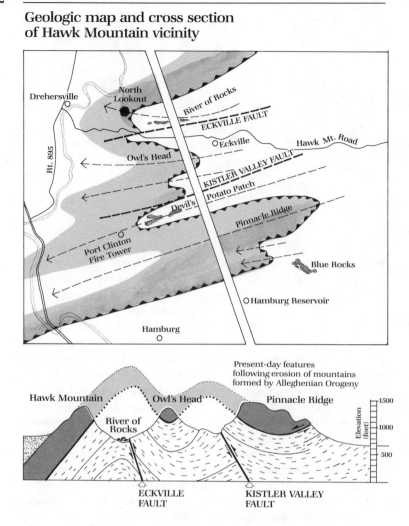

the process of breakdown began. Brittle rocks breached the surface during folding and broke open on the summits of folds, exposing the weak shales beneath. Differential erosion proceeded, and weaker materials were carried into an ocean whose beach now faced east. Quartzites were resistant to weathering, and they remain today the high points of the Appalachian Mountain chain.

Mountain-building activity has been at a standstill in the region, then, for the past 225 million years. Erosional forces have been attacking the Appalachians ever since, reducing their stature and moving their sediments into the Atlantic

Ocean, where they await another orogeny to push them skyward.

Two landforms in the immediate area deserve particular mention: the River of Rocks and the Donat. Prominent on the landscape, each is important geologically and each serves as a reference point for hawk-watchers to point out positions of migrating birds of prey.

## The River of Rocks

Below the South Lookout is a large boulder field—the River of Rocks—a mile-long tumble of thousands of large boulders, some of them twenty feet in diameter. This impressive jumble of rocks arrived close to its present position during the last glacial period, the Wisconsin.

The continental ice sheet never quite reached Hawk Mountain, its ultimate front being located about forty-five miles north, on the Pocono Plateau. But during the glacial period Hawk Mountain experienced frequent snowfalls and frosts. With the freezes and thaws of a ten-thousand-year-long winter, the character of the massive boulders was bound to change. Water trapped in the rocks froze and cracked the rocks apart along their depositional planes. Those boulders now resting in the valley originated on the ridgetop near the South Lookout. They moved to their present position by sliding over the underlying Martinsburg shale, coming to rest as tongues of blocks stretched over the ice and mud. This process is called solifluction. When the glacier retreated, about eleven thousand years ago, temperatures moderated and over time rains washed away the shale debris, exposing the boulder field.

Farther into the valley, small peninsulas of forest invade the farmland. This configuration occurs where tongues of sliding rocks came down off the mountain to rest in the valley and, over the years, gathered soil and vegetation. They remain forested because they cannot be plowed. The River of Rocks has not yet been claimed by the forest, but eventually it will be. Beneath the boulder field runs a small stream that carries the materials of Hawk Mountain inexorably toward the sea.

## The Donat

To the east, in the valley, is a landform that resembles an ancient volcanic cinder cone. The Donat or Donat's Peak—named for the family who formerly owned the property—is used by hawk-watchers as a point of reference during the fall

The River of Rocks

Joseph Snook

migration to locate hawks moving out across the valley toward the Pinnacle, a promontory on the ridge east of the North Lookout. A prominent landmark on the Shochary Ridge, one of a series of low ridges dipping away at low angles to the east, the Donat is composed of Martinsburg shale overlaid by Ordovician sandstones formed about 450 million years ago.

# CHAPTER 3

# The Living Mountain

Since the continental glacier retreated north, the living mountain has undergone extensive changes. The ice and snow gave way to a spruce-fir forest; but as the continent warmed, broadleaved trees moved north and the boreal forest retreated poleward. A variety of topography-dependent habitats developed. Tulip trees thrived in the moist lowlands and on south-facing slopes; hemlocks flourished in cool, north-facing ravines; and oaks dominated the drier ridgetops.

The forest where the sanctuary is located was largely intact in the seventeenth century. An approximation of what is comprised can be found in Victor Shelford's classic, *The Ecology of North America,* in which he attempted to reconstruct an undisturbed Appalachian forest. He hypothesized that a chunk of primeval forest about the size of Hawk Mountain Sanctuary would contain 750,000 mature trees of 24 species, and beneath them an equal number of seedlings, some 3 million shrubs, and 230 to 460 million herbaceous plants.

Shelford postulated a summer population of about 27 billion insects and spiders, which would provide food for nearly 8,000 pairs of small birds and their young. The great horned owl, barred owl, red-tailed hawk, broad-winged hawk, and red-shouldered hawk—the chief avian predators in the forest—would average 3 individuals per 75,000 trees. Rodents, mostly white-footed mice, would abound, averaging perhaps 350,000—or about 1 mouse for every 2 trees. White-tailed deer populations would vary greatly, but in this hypothetical forest, 400 is the optimal herd size.

Pretty impressive statistics.

In 1934, when the sanctuary was founded, the woodland was far from primeval. Repeated timbering, followed by burning, had reduced the forest to scrub oak saplings. For more than a half-century now, however, the forest has been little manipulated by humans, and once again it approaches Shelford's hypothetical Appalachian forest.

Of the several recent instruments of change at work in the forest, the most drastic in effect was the accidental introduction of the chestnut blight. First discovered in New York City in 1904, and apparently imported on chestnut trees or seeds from the Orient, this fungal disease attacks bark and the tissues beneath, choking the transport system that carries nutrients to and from the roots and leaves. Spores of the fungus were carried west and south by the wind, spreading the disease. The American chestnut—monarch of the Appalachian forest—had no defense against the blight, and by 1935 all had been killed as far south as Kentucky. American chestnuts continue to sprout from the roots of long-fallen trees, but the saplings are quickly blighted, and they seldom survive to reach heights of more than fifteen feet.

The forest ecosystem wherein the sanctuary is located is known to ecologists as a mixed deciduous forest of broad-leaved trees. Within this forest are about 25 species of trees that shed their foliage each autumn. Just before this annual sloughing off, the forest canopy is transformed from green to a flaming array of reds, russets, yellows, and oranges—one of the most striking phenomena in nature. Taken for granted by most residents, the Appalachian forest's annual coloration is unsurpassed anywhere in the world.

Occurring with the rich diversity of broad-leaved trees is an impressive diversity of other plants and accompanying fauna, making the Appalachian forest a land of great interest and beauty. Naturalists of every persuasion have explored the forest, finding it home to about 3,000 species of higher plants, 50 species of mammals, 390 species of resident and seasonal birds, 106 species of reptiles and amphibians, and 263 species of fish.

## Approaching the Sanctuary

Hawk Mountain Sanctuary encompasses twenty-four hundred acres. Elevations range from 600 feet above sea level along the lower stretches of Kettle Creek to 1,550 feet near the North Lookout. Several important habitats are identified on the folding map at the back of the book and are discussed below. The sanctuary trail system, also shown on the map, enables visitors to enter these habitats. Two nearby areas of special interest, the Pine Swamp and the Little Schuylkill River, are accessible by road or foot. In appendix 3 is a checklist of the more common plants and animals found on the sanctuary and in adjacent areas.

Most visitors approach the sanctuary by driving up Hawk Mountain Road from the north and west. The road crosses the Little Schuylkill River near Drehersville, where Maurice Broun lived when he took up warden duties on the mountain. This

Maurice Broun

A dead hawk suspended from a bridge in Drehersville to taunt Maurice Broun

tiny village was a whistle-stop on the Reading Railroad. Up until the early 1950s a steel-girder bridge, since replaced, crossed the river. It was from that bridge that residents of Drehersville suspended dead hawks to taunt the new warden as he walked the two miles uphill to the sanctuary.

The Little Schuylkill itself has undergone remarkable changes in the past century. Since 1850 the river has passed several important anthracite coal operations as it meandered south. Polluted for many years with repeated doses of acid mine water and tons of silt, the river was biologically dead until the late 1960s. In the 1950s the Army Corps of Engineers dredged the river as part of a massive flood-control program. While the exercise cleaned the river bed, it did little to buffer the water's acidity.

Before the river was silted up and acidified, it had supported an important shad fishery. Shad migrated to the upper stretches to spawn until dams were built north of Philadelphia. Under pressure from the Pennsylvania Department of Environmental Resources and the Pennsylvania Fish Commission in the late 1960s, mine operators began to neutralize their acid waste before it entered the Little Schuylkill River, which subsequently made a remarkable recovery. From the North Lookout, osprey can now be seen fishing along the river. Fly fishermen wade the shallows, and Canada geese raise their families along the banks. In 1989 the state registered the river system north of the Kittatinny Ridge under the Pennsylvania Scenic Rivers Act.

Just after Hawk Mountain Road crosses the river, on the way to the sanctuary, a gravel road to the left ascends the river cliffs, which are covered with dense rhododendron tangles. Along the sanctuary's northern boundary are a series of seasonal pools, where in spring and fall visitors may encounter waves of migrating warblers: bay-breasted, orange-crowned, chestnut-sided, and worm-eating, to name just a few. It is not uncommon to record fifteen species in one visit during these seasonal pulses. The boglike pools are home to several species of salamanders, and growing among clumps of sphagnum moss is the sundew, a tiny insectivorous plant. Each spring a chorus of peepers and wood frogs sings there.

From the east, the approach to the sanctuary is less dramatic. Nevertheless, commanding views of the Kittatinny Ridge can be had along Hawk Mountain Road. The major town in the area is Kempton, a bustling rail depot at the turn of the century that was best known for the large quantities of potatoes shipped from the freight station. At Albright's Mill, the center of present-day activity, farmers from the surrounding country-side sell their crops. Wheat, corn, and soybeans grown in the shadow of Hawk Mountain find their way via Kempton to grain elevators in Philadelphia and Baltimore for export around the world. In addition to grain crops, other important local farm products are milk, potatoes, and Christmas trees.

The village encountered along Hawk Mountain Road before entering the sanctuary from the east is Eckville. (*Eck* is Pennsylvania German for "corner.") At one time this thriving village featured an active ice dam, a grocery store, and a post office, not to mention a hex doctor and a witch. Eckville was the home of the Jacob Gerhardt family, whose role in the history of Hawk Mountain was chronicled in chapter 1.

In Eckville gravel-covered Pine Swamp Road turns left off Hawk Mountain Road and travels south. In a half mile the road passes the parking areas of the State Game Lands. A walk through the Game Lands can yield many sightings of spring and fall warblers. Both golden-winged and blue-winged warblers nest in the fields above Pine Swamp Road, and their hybrids are sometimes sighted there. Flocks of wild turkeys may be seen as well. Visitors should be aware of the local hunting seasons before entering the Game Lands.

The Pine Swamp—actually a wet bottomland rather than a swamp—has interesting faunal and botanical characteristics. On the south side of the road, along Rausch's Creek, are groves of hemlock and tangles of rhododendron, both typical of cool, north-facing slopes. The land beyond Rausch's Creek is private, but a walk along Pine Swamp Road in search of birds, especially owls, can be very productive. On misty, moonlit nights throughout the year four species of owls—barred, northern saw-whet, great horned, and eastern screech—can be heard, the first three to the south and the last from the grassy meadow north of the road, where it is easily called. On occasion, during late winter and early spring, the wild screams of a bobcat can be heard coming from the slope of the Pinnacle.

The Pine Swamp figures prominently in folklore about the supernatural. Still-unsolved murders have occurred there, and local residents tell stories of devils appearing on hazy summer evenings. A cave on top of the Pinnacle is the reputed den of a dragon that flies out across the valley toward Kempton.

Pine Swamp Road continues east, eventually rejoining Hawk Mountain Road three miles east of the sanctuary.

## The Sanctuary Trails

### The Lookout Trail

The Lookout Trail, beginning at the Visitor Center, leads through second-growth oak forest to the North Lookout, an easy three-quarters-of-a-mile walk. From the entrance gate it is a short distance to the first observation point: the South Lookout. There visitors can look over the forest some seven hundred feet below to a patchwork quilt of farmland. A lovely panorama stretches to the far horizon forty-five miles to the east. When southerly and easterly winds prevail, the South Lookout is a good vantage point to observe migrating raptors. It is staffed by sanctuary naturalists each weekend from September through November.

The chestnut oak is the dominant tree along the Lookout Trail. It favors high, dry ridgetops and is tolerant of poor soils and exposure to the elements, especially wind. The most stressful time is winter, when storms may leave an inch-thick accumulation of ice on the branches. Other canopy and understory trees are found among the chestnut oaks. Among the more common are red maple, black gum, sassafras, shadbush, fire cherry, pitch pine, and witch hazel, whose yellow, spidery blossoms are the last to bloom in the fall. The most common shrubs are sheep laurel and several species of blueberry and huckleberry.

In the late 1960s the gypsy moth began to invade this section of the Appalachians. Its voracious caterpillars, which have a preference for oak leaves, completely defoliated the sanctuary in 1972. Subsequent defoliations have weakened many species of trees, particularly the oaks. Along the trails and lookouts are numerous dead trees, killed by disease after defoliations reduced their resistance. The gypsy moth, however, has become a permanent member of the forest ecosystem, and today parasites and predators have established themselves and can effectively control the gypsy moth as long as its population does not reach epidemic proportions. Even then, the swollen population will collapse as a result of starvation and disease.

Before the trail climbs to the Slide and the Hall of the Mountain King, the beautiful pink lady's slipper, or moccasin flower, can be found in the spring. The well-drained, acidic, sandy soil provides a suitable environment for this lovely orchid. It reaches full bloom in late May and early June.

Among the showy plants demanding attention along the trail are rhododendron and mountain laurel. Rhododendrons occur frequently on the higher elevations of the trail, especially at the Slide and around the North Lookout. The laurel, Pennsylvania's state flower, reaches its peak bloom in early June. Some years it blooms more luxuriantly than others, but the showy white and pink blossoms are always lovely. Rhododendron flowers appear later in June. Both the Little Schuylkill River and Pine Swamp areas have magnificent rhododendron blooms as well; but at a thousand feet lower, the blooms there can occur a bit earlier.

Two side trails also lead to the North Lookout. The Escarpment Trail turns right off the Lookout Trail north of the South Lookout. This demanding trail, leading along the edge of the escarpment, offers excellent views of the valley. The Express Trail, which breaks off to the right farther along the Lookout Trail, is a shortcut to the North Lookout. Just short of the ridge summit is a charcoal flat on the left of the Express Trail, silent testimony to an early mountaintop industry. The charcoal produced here was used to fuel a blacksmith's forge near the Slide operated in conjunction with sand quarrying at the turn of the century (see chapter 1).

The Hall of the Mountain King

Maurice Broun, impressed by the cathedral hemlocks and steep cliffs along the section of trail leading from the Slide to the summit of the North Lookout, named the area the Hall of the Mountain King after Edvard Grieg's *Peer Gynt* Suite no. 1. The Hall vividly illustrates the role geological forces have played in shaping the Appalachian Mountains. Here is displayed the collision of continental land masses during the Alleghenian Orogeny. Tilted rocks can be seen on all the exposed outcrops along the ridge, but nowhere as dramatically as in the Hall.

The North Lookout

The North Lookout has been visited by more than a million people, including many of the world's famous naturalists; indeed, this lookout has been called the "crossroads of naturalists." Although the major attraction has always been the annual fall migration of birds of prey, the North Lookout is visited throughout the year by people with a variety of interests.

In spring, especially during the second and third weeks of May, an impressive warbler migration occurs along the north flank of the mountain, and quite a few species can be recorded on a single May morning. The spring raptor migration is not remarkable at Hawk Mountain.

Among other birds, pileated woodpeckers are often heard or seen flying below the lookout. These crow-sized woodpeckers nest on the lower elevations of the sanctuary. There is a healthy population of great horned owls in the forest on both sides of the lookout. Seldom seen, these big owls are heard at night throughout the year from the lookout. In the fall the hawk-watcher who perseveres until day's end may hear a pair of these owls dueting just off the lookout.

The North Lookout features several plants of special interest. The American mountain ash—a very large specimen grows on the north side of the lookout—thrives on the north side of most exposed outcroppings throughout the central Appalachian Mountains. Unspectacular for most of the year, the tree is a blaze of color come fall. The berries begin to turn with early frosts, and by October's end they are bright red. Even with the lookout full of visitors, the mountain ash is visited by blue jays,

cedar waxwings, chipmunks, and red squirrels, all of which feed heavily on ripened berries. When bouts of frost alternate with warm days the berries ferment. On rare occasions cedar waxwings will gorge on fermented berries, after which they may fly about drunkenly, bouncing off people and rocks.

Toward the prow of the lookout is a small, dome-shaped, shrub, known by botanists as *Nemopanthus mucronata*. A species of mountain holly that grows primarily in swampy bogs, it is a remnant of the boreal forest. Only a few individuals occur on the sanctuary. Several species of deciduous mountain holly grow on the North Lookout. They are cataloged in the checklist.

Those who spend some time on the lookout will undoubtedly encounter a small, rufous-colored rodent scampering about among the backpacks and picnic baskets. Red-backed voles have delighted visitors since hawk watching began here. In fact, this vole lived here along with saber-toothed cats and woolly mammoths during the Pleistocene epoch. Red-backed voles become quite tame and are bold enough to enter packs and lunch bags in search of food. One visitor returned to his motel room after a full day of hawk watching on the North Lookout to discover an energetic red-backed vole in the bottom of his pack basket. He took the vole home to the lookout next morning.

Years ago another, much larger rodent, the eastern woodrat, was common among the rockslides on the lookouts. Unhappily, they have long since been extirpated from the sanctuary and surrounding mountain lands. No one really knows why.

## The Skyline Trail

Hikers who climb about three hundred feet down the face of the outcrop off the front of the North Lookout will encounter the Skyline Trail (blue blaze). This trail connects the Appalachian Trail with the other sanctuary trails. Persons entering the sanctuary along the Skyline Trail are responsible for an admission fee upon arrival at the North Lookout or the Visitor Center.

## The River of Rocks Trail

The River of Rocks Trail winds through the sanctuary's greatest diversity of plants and animals. Beginning at the halfway

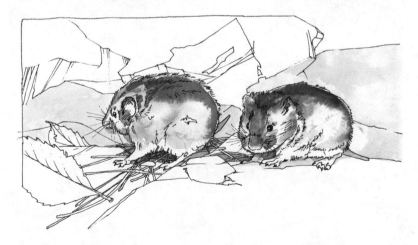

point between the two lookouts and running eastward, the River of Rocks Trail descends abruptly over the escarpment, crosses the Golden Eagle Trail, and continues deeper and deeper into the valley. Hikers on this trail are treated to one of the most beautiful areas of the sanctuary. The thick groves of rhododendron and rich variety of trees offer pleasant contrast to the high, dry, oak-covered ridgetops. Along the way hints of the large boulder field can be seen through the forest. Near the eastern end of the sanctuary, Kettle Creek emerges from beneath the River of Rocks and tumbles to lower elevations, eventually joining Pine Creek in Eckville. This area is delicate and ecologically sensitive. *Visitors must remain on the trail at all times.*

A winter walk here is especially exciting: many of the sanctuary's elusive animals can be identified from their tracks in the snow. The secretive bobcat hunts among the rhododendron

The River of Rocks

W. R. Fink, Jr.

thickets for grouse and rabbits, as does the gray fox. A resident flock of wild turkeys frequents the area, and their large tracks crisscross the length of the trail. Tracks of deer mice and voles are usually visible along the creek banks. A large herd of white-tailed deer lives in this section of the sanctuary as well. Since 1985 two mammals previously not present on the sanctuary—black bear and coyote—have appeared, and their numbers are increasing. They or their tracks can best be observed along the River of Rocks Trail.

Spring comes to the lower stretches of the sanctuary a week or two before it arrives on top. Among the early migrant birds to return to Hawk Mountain is the eastern phoebe, whose plaintive notes can be heard throughout the forest in April. An early spring walk is delightful. The musty fragrances of a spring forest are invigorating. There are numerous shallow pools along Kettle Creek that contain brook trout, whose brightly colored males are especially striking. (Brook trout are also found in Rausch's Creek along Pine Swamp Road.) These natives of the Appalachian aquatic ecosystem never grow very large. They feed on adult and nymphal stoneflies, caddisflies, and mayflies. Only clean streams support brook trout, and local populations are abundant and healthy. Kettle Creek is usually high during spring; care should be taken when crossing it.

On either side of the creek ferns poke their fiddleheads above the leaf litter. Just as brook trout indicate clean water, so an abundance of ferns indicates a healthy forest. The many species of ferns growing on the sanctuary are cited in the checklist.

An early morning walk to the River of Rocks during late spring or early summer will find the resident songbirds in full chorus. A good place to sit is out on the boulders themselves. The River of Rocks provides a natural opening in the forest, and birds are attracted to the forest edge on either side. Rufous-sided towhees, ovenbirds, rose-breasted grosbeaks, scarlet tanagers, northern orioles, and red-eyed vireos are but a few of the species that nest in the area. Several pairs of broad-winged hawks nest on the sanctuary each season, and their shrill whistles sound above the forest from early spring into late summer. As summer progresses, young broadwings can be seen testing the thermal air currents that develop above the boulder field.

In the midsection of the boulder field, near the eastern junction of the Golden Eagle and River of Rocks trails, is a curious hole. The rocks here were removed long ago to provide access to the water flowing beneath, which was used in a steam-powered sawmill located a hundred yards to the east.

Obviously it would be impossible to treat—or even to men-

tion—all the inhabitants of the sanctuary's forest. To supplement this summary, the checklist (appendix 3) details the variety of plant and animal species found here. Private walks along the trails will be largely adventures in self-instruction. For additional education, the sanctuary schedules guided forays throughout the year. Members of the Hawk Mountain Sanctuary Association receive notice of these events in *Hawk Mountain News*, a semiannual periodical. Visitors and friends are encouraged to become members of the association, not only to keep abreast of seasonal activities but also to help with the ongoing tasks of protecting and maintaining the sanctuary. Those interested in becoming members can write to Hawk Mountain Sanctuary Association, Route 2, Kempton, PA 19529, or can call the sanctuary at (215) 756-6961. The sanctuary is open every day, except Christmas Day and New Year's Day, from 8:00 A.M. to 5:00 P.M.

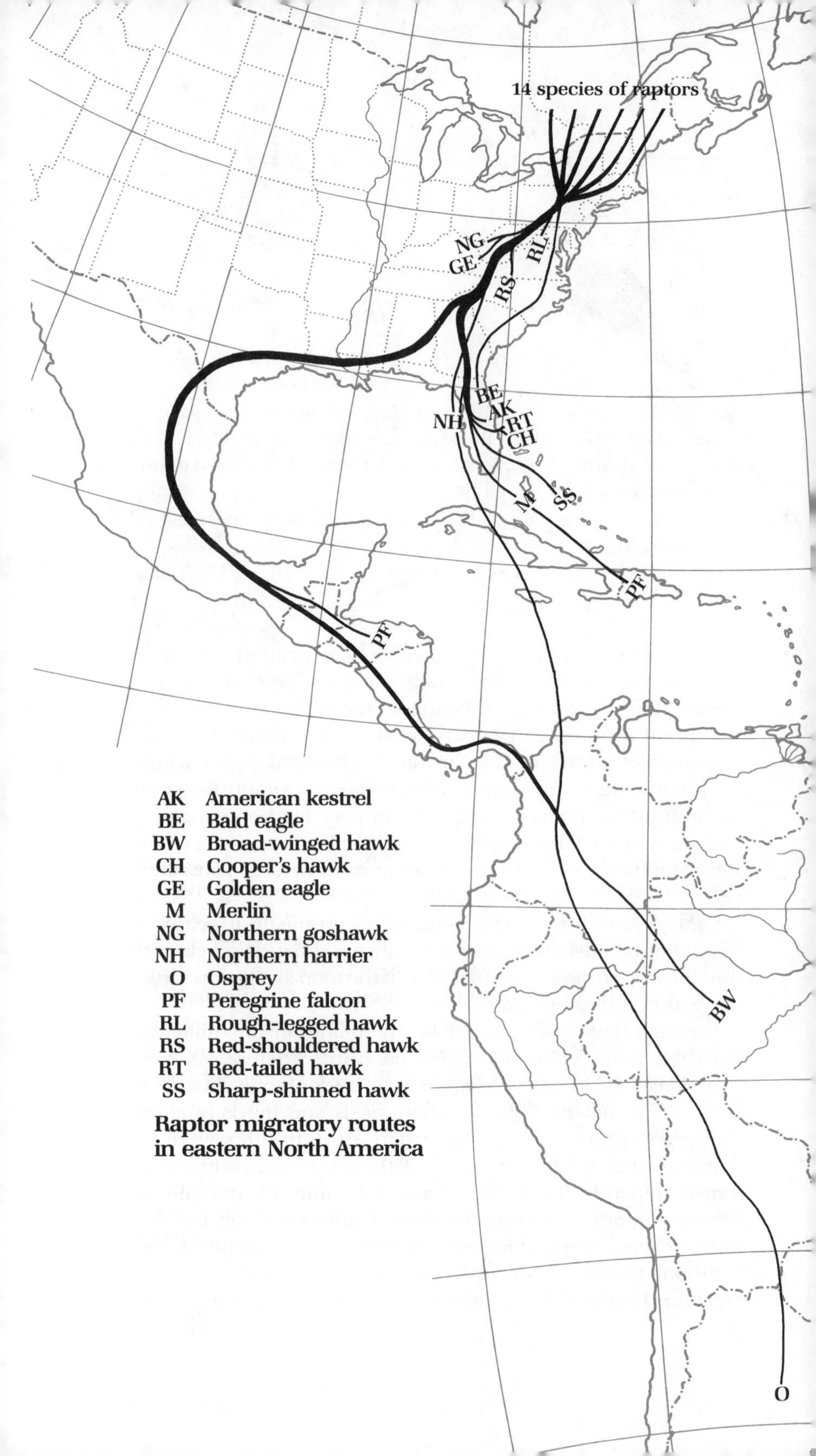

14 species of raptors

NG Northern goshawk
GE Golden eagle
RL Rough-legged hawk
RS Red-shouldered hawk
BE Bald eagle
AK American kestrel
NH Northern harrier
RT Red-tailed hawk
CH Cooper's hawk
M Merlin
SS Sharp-shinned hawk
PF Peregrine falcon
BW Broad-winged hawk
O Osprey

AK   American kestrel
BE   Bald eagle
BW   Broad-winged hawk
CH   Cooper's hawk
GE   Golden eagle
M    Merlin
NG   Northern goshawk
NH   Northern harrier
O    Osprey
PF   Peregrine falcon
RL   Rough-legged hawk
RS   Red-shouldered hawk
RT   Red-tailed hawk
SS   Sharp-shinned hawk

**Raptor migratory routes
in eastern North America**

# CHAPTER 4

# Out of the North

Twice each year there occurs a massive movement of billions of the world's birds between breeding grounds and wintering areas. In North America, migration is generally oriented north-south because most migratory species move south in the fall to escape the rigors of winter and then fly north in spring to breed. In other locations, the shifts are east-west or elevational. The most dramatic movements are those that cross whole continents or even hemispheres.

Migratory movements are largely a response to seasonal change in the availability of food. (The life cycles and dietary preferences of the raptors that migrate over Hawk Mountain are summarized in appendix 1.) Some birds feed primarily on cold-blooded prey, and as the temperature drops and the prey die or prepare to overwinter in inaccessible locations, the birds are forced to move to areas where an abundance of food will ensure their survival. Broad-winged hawks, for example, feed largely on reptiles, amphibians, and small rodents. With the approach of winter in the Northeast, chemical codes within the broadwing's brain trigger an impulse to move south—some as far south as Bolivia. Some birds of prey feed on songbirds and shorebirds, following them as they migrate to areas where their food is plentiful. Frozen lakes and rivers force fish-eating raptors to seek open water.

Some raptors are nomadic, wandering erratically in search of food. Red-tailed hawks may move just a short distance from their nesting grounds, for instance. If the food supply dwindles there, they will move again.

Humans have been fascinated by migration for millennia. Early humans were migratory creatures themselves, and knowledge of animal migration was undoubtedly linked to survival. By moving to areas where birds and herds of mammals concentrated during migration, early hunters were assured an abundant food supply. Although human survival no longer depends on these movements, hints of atavistic response remain. Whose pulse doesn't quicken when the first skein of geese "honks" its way north in an early spring sky?

Among the earliest recorded accounts of migration are several found in the Old Testament. In Job 39:26 it is written, "Doth the hawk fly by thy wisdom, and stretch her wings toward the south?" The prophet Jeremiah (8:7) referred to the migration of birds when he wrote, "Yea, the stork in the heaven knoweth her appointed times; and the turtle[dove] and the crane and the swallow observe the time of their coming; but my people know not the judgment of the Lord."

## Studying Migration

Bird migration raises several intriguing questions: How and when did it originate? Why do some migrants fly from the Arctic to the Antarctic and back each year, while others travel no more than a few tens of miles from their breeding grounds? Why do some species fly only at night, others only during the day, still others night and day? How can a three-month-old Alaska-hatched shorebird find its way, without adult guidance, to the tip of Africa and then return? Ornithologists have long been puzzled by such questions, but despite a century of dedicated work they have many more plausible theories than certain answers.

Researchers grapple with the fundamental issues of migration in both laboratory and field. Laboratory workers study such phenomena as the hormonal mechanisms that trigger migration, the navigational cues the migrants employ, and the metabolic expense of migration. Using aluminum leg rings to mark individuals and radar to track whole flocks across the sky, teams of ornithologists in the field identify migration pathways and stopovers, and they study such things as the influence of weather on migration and the feeding and resting behavior of migrants.

A simple and inexpensive way to study migration is to watch birds as they move past a single location that concentrates large numbers of migrants. What makes this method attractive is that anyone with a little training can participate. Although it is difficult to standardize data gathered by a large number of observers using a variety of techniques under different weather conditions, observing from a single concentration point is one of the best ways to study migrating birds of prey.

Still, such study of raptor migration didn't begin until Maurice Broun first climbed to Hawk Mountain's North Lookout in September of 1934 to record the passage of birds of prey. It has since, literally, spread throughout the world. Since 1934 many other raptor migration concentration points have been identified. The map on page 46 locates a few of these hot spots and shows in a general way the courses of raptors in the

Northeast. Every year thousands of people climb to ridgetop hawk watches. Many others position themselves along lake, bay, and ocean shores. The hawk-watching community, a network comprising mostly dedicated amateurs, collects hundreds of thousands of bits of information each season. The Hawk Migration Association of North America was founded in 1974 to gather and process data from hawk-watching stations throughout the continent. With this great wealth of data—detailing where, when, which birds, how many, how high, and in what weather—hawk watching is making an important contribution to the study of bird migration.

While counting the numbers of raptors migrating under a variety of weather conditions, hawk-watchers have recorded many other observations over years of study. Whether birds of prey feed while migrating has been much debated, and this question has led observers to look more closely at passing migrants to determine if their crops are distended. When a raptor swallows its prey, the food first enters a saclike organ above the stomach, called the crop. The prey expands the crop, stretching the skin and pushing the upper breast feathers outward. This swollen area can be seen by trained observers. At Hawk Mountain sharp-shinned and Cooper's hawks are often seen flying past lookouts with full crops, having taken advantage of migrating songbirds along the ridge. Migrant red-tailed hawks often hover above the forest in a hunting posture, and they, too, pass with swollen crops. Broad-winged hawks and American kestrels have been seen snatching migrating monarch butterflies and dragonflies and eating them on the wing. Occasionally a passing osprey totes a fish.

Hawk Mountain remains one of the premier hawk-watching locations in the world. Excluding 1943–1945, the years of Maurice Broun's military service, raptors have been counted and recorded here virtually every fall day (downpour days excepted) since 1934. The results represent the greatest bank of raptor migration data ever collected (see appendix 2). From late August until early December each year, an average of about twenty thousand birds of prey of fourteen species use the Kittatinny Ridge on their way south.

## Conditions for Migration

Generally, bird migration takes place on a broad front like that of a weather system, rather than along distinct corridors. But en route, migrants may encounter topographic features in the form of coasts or mountain ridges that concentrate and

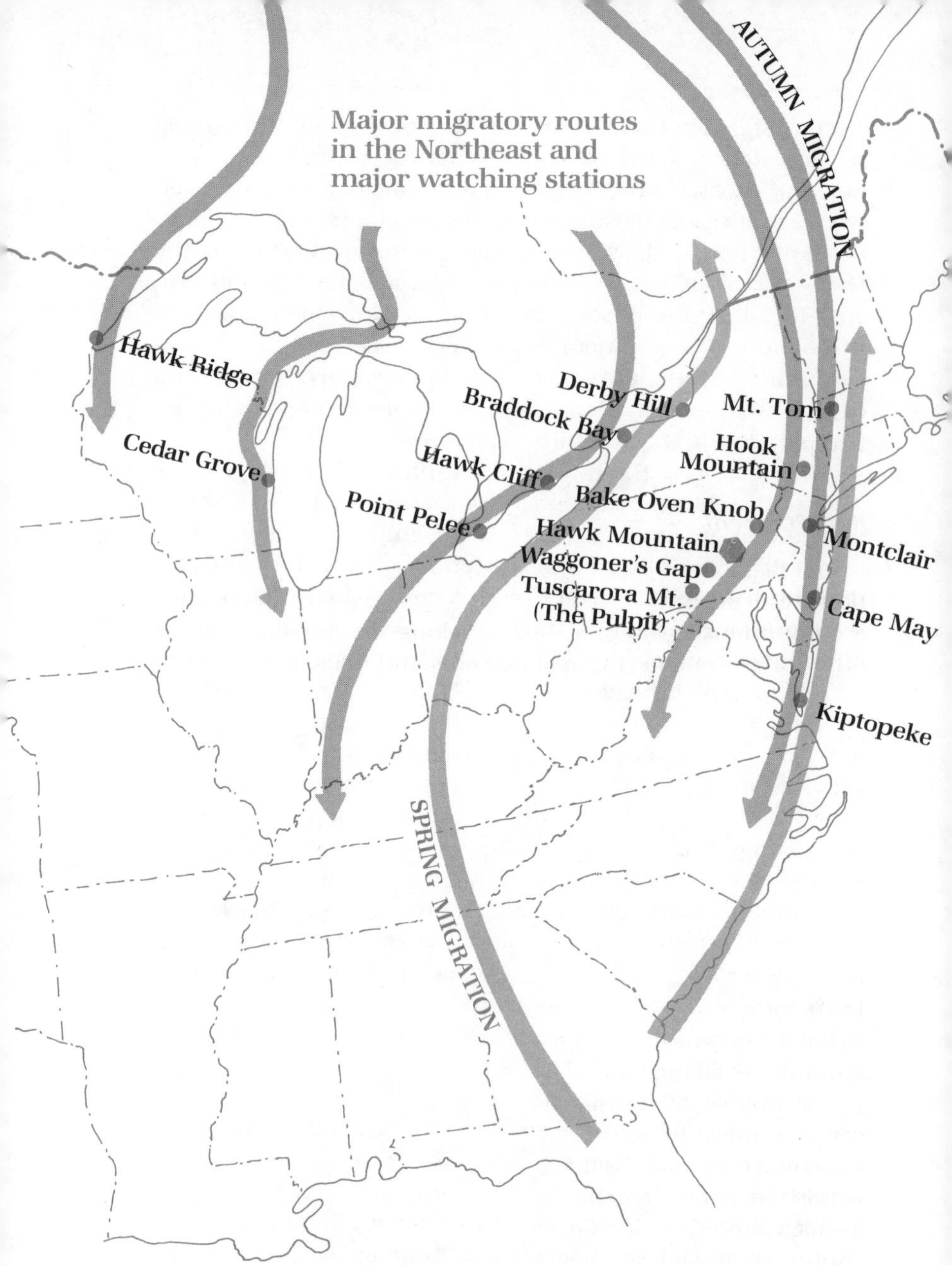

Major migratory routes in the Northeast and major watching stations

AUTUMN MIGRATION

Hawk Ridge

Cedar Grove

Point Pelee

Hawk Cliff

Braddock Bay

Derby Hill

Mt. Tom

Hook Mountain

Bake Oven Knob

Hawk Mountain

Waggoner's Gap

Tuscarora Mt. (The Pulpit)

Montclair

Cape May

Kiptopeke

SPRING MIGRATION

direct the birds; biologists call these barriers *leading lines*. Some species, including some raptors, readily fly across large lakes or bays, even open ocean. But for the most part birds of prey tend to migrate over land, where mountain ridges serve as important leading lines. The air currents associated with mountain ridges allow migrating hawks to conserve energy during flight, and hawks will follow these ridges as long as they point in the general direction of migration.

Hawks coming from eastern Canada fly on a broad front over New England and New York. When the wind is in the north-to-west quarter of the compass, many raptors drift southwest across the grain of the Appalachians until they reach the Kittatinny Ridge, the ridge where Hawk Mountain is located. Oriented northeast to southwest, the Kittatinny is the southernmost ridge in the northern Appalachian Mountains. At the Kittatinny raptors often angle right and head southwest, avoiding the large expanses of open land south of the ridge. In other words, under ideal conditions raptors pile up along the ridge and parade south along a narrow corridor.

## Ridge Currents

The flight dynamics, timing, and methods of raptor migration are all influenced by air currents. Two types of air currents are important to hawks migrating along the Appalachians or other ridge systems: thermal currents and deflected currents.

### Thermal Air Currents

Thermals are generated as the sun's heat warms the south side of a mountain ridge, for example, or a plowed field or a rock outcrop. The warm air near the surface begins to expand and pushes up against the cooler air above. For a while the situation is somewhat akin to a pot of water nearing a boil, with the bubble of warm air held down by the cooler, heavier air above. But if conditions are right, the thermal bubble eventually rises from the ground, sucking cooler air in behind it—from, for example, a nearby north-facing ridge. The bubble of rising air can be widely extended or narrowly localized, and around it is falling air—downdrafts.

The bubble of warm air continues to expand as it rises, carrying moisture with it. Gradually it loses heat to the surrounding cooler air. As the temperatures equalize, water vapor within the bubble reaches its condensation point and a cloud forms. Cumulus clouds mark the tops of thermals, whose lift continues as long as they are supplied with warm air from below. The billowing clouds rise higher and higher before disintegrating and vanishing.

The production of thermals is greatest in the spring, when the sun's rays strike the earth's surface at the most advantageous angle. In northern North America thermal production is also strong in early fall, but by late autumn thermal activity slows dramatically as the sun's angle becomes more oblique.

Wide-winged buteos, or soaring hawks, use thermals to good

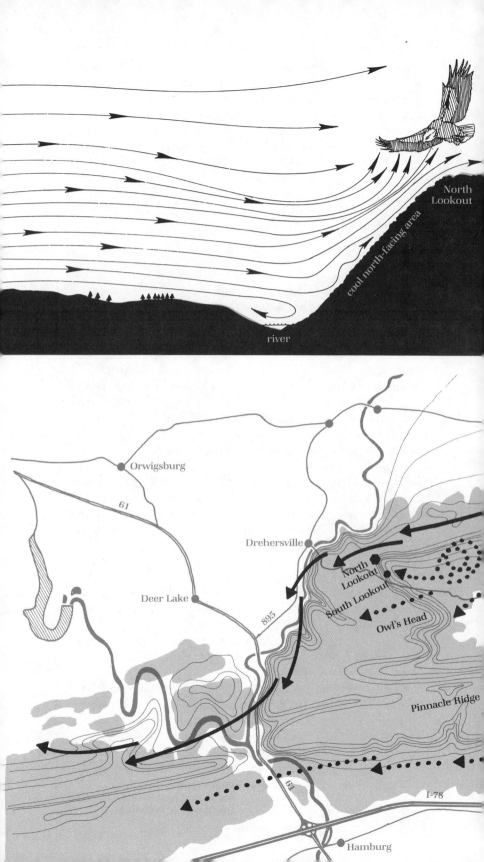

North
Lookout

cool north-facing area

river

Orwigsburg

61

Drehersville

Deer Lake

895

North
Lookout

South Lookout

Owl's Head

Pinnacle Ridge

61

I-78

Hamburg

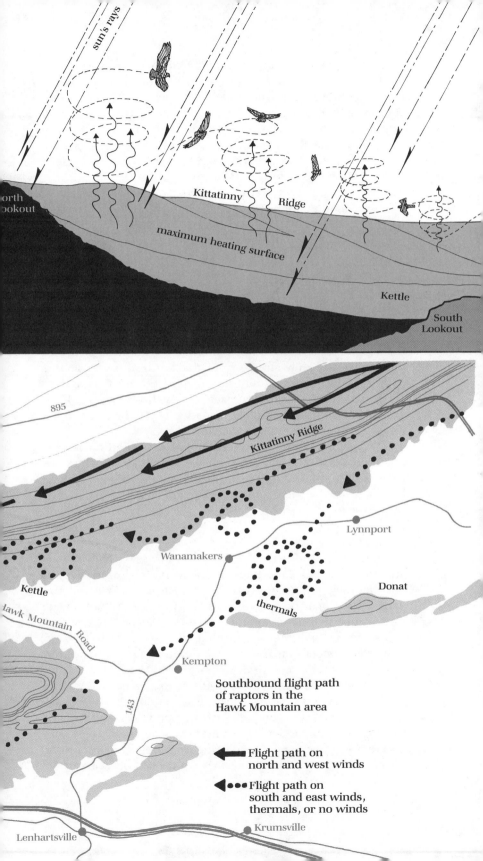

sun's rays

Kittatinny      Ridge

maximum heating surface

North
Lookout

Kettle

South
Lookout

895

Kittatinny Ridge

Lynnport

Wanamakers

Kettle

Donat

Hawk Mountain Road

thermals

143

Kempton

Southbound flight path
of raptors in the
Hawk Mountain area

→ Flight path on
north and west winds

◄•••  Flight path on
south and east winds,
thermals, or no winds

Lenhartsville

Krumsville

advantage, and the broad-winged hawk, a master soarer, is king of the thermal. During the peak of the broadwing migration in mid-September, great movements of these hawks are seen. Hawk-watchers refer to a flock of swirling broadwings as a "kettle"—because of the boiling appearance of the flock in the thermal bubble. Broadwings use thermal air currents as their main aid to travel all the way from the woodlands of eastern North America to Central and South America.

When a thermal begins to develop, dust, leaves, insects—anything light enough to be drawn into the rising air mass—can be carried aloft with the warm, moist air. Broadwings evidently detect the development of thermals by sighting the upward movement of the materials within the bubble, and move toward it. It is not uncommon to see upward of a hundred birds in a single kettle in the Northeast, and thousands at a time are occasionally recorded.

Broadwings are lofted higher and higher, until they reach the point where the thermal begins to lose energy. By then the birds have sighted another thermal—with birds or debris within it—and they stream from the top of the bubble and glide downward, losing altitude, toward the next rising column, which lofts them once again. This hopscotching from one thermal to another allows broadwings to travel great distances without expending much energy.

Although red-shouldered hawks and red-tailed hawks are also buteos, they utilize thermal air currents on migration far less than do broadwings, in part because thermal activity begins to wane before most redtails and redshoulders push southward.

### Deflected Air Currents

Many species of ridge-flying raptors also use deflected air currents at Hawk Mountain. Such currents—updrafts—are best here when a northerly or northwesterly wind strikes the flank of the ridge and rides up and over the top. Updrafts occur throughout the fall as long as the wind blows. Easterly and southerly winds are also deflected, but the deflected northwesterlies concentrate the greatest number of hawks along the ridge.

Southbound hawks use the updrafts to give them lift while they use gravity to drive them forward at 60 miles per hour. They glide mile after mile on outstretched wings and can cut their sail-surface enough to maintain a steady balance in relation to the lifting power of the rising air. Much as a surfer rides the crest of a wave of water, birds ride the crest of a wave of air.

On an ideal day, a raptor flying at an average speed of 40 mph can travel 250 miles or more.

When the productive winds prevail, the best viewing is from north-facing outcrops along the ridge. The stronger the wind, the closer the hawks fly to the ridge in order to avoid air turbulence. In very strong winds many hawks fold their wings and literally plummet through the air, without losing altitude.

## Weather Patterns

John Haugh's 1972 doctoral dissertation for Cornell University presents the results of his study of the relationship between weather and the eastern raptor migration. Haugh identified five principal weather conditions associated with the concentration of birds along a ridge during September, October, and November:

1. the recent passage of a low-pressure system,
2. northerly or westerly winds,
3. decreasing temperatures,
4. increasing barometric pressures, and
5. decreasing humidity.

In contrast, raptors will migrate in significant numbers along a ridge during March and April when the following conditions exist:

1. the approach of a low-pressure system,
2. southerly winds,
3. increasing temperatures, and
4. decreasing barometric pressure.

It would seem that one could, by checking weather maps, predict a good day to be on the ridge, watching for hawks. Sometimes that works, but not always, especially during mid-September when broad-winged hawks are migrating. Often this species seems to ignore weather patterns.

Sanctuary records suggest that the major ingredients for a successful fall day at Hawk Mountain are

1. the passage of a low-pressure system to the north across New York or the New England states,
2. an advancing cold front moving down from the Great Lakes or Canada, and
3. two or three consecutive days of northerly winds.

The combination of all three factors produces the best flights.

When a high-pressure cell becomes stationary over the Northeast, especially in September or early October, balmy, windless weather ensues. On these days, flying hawks tend to scatter over the valleys, bypassing the ridges completely, or they may simply wait until the next major weather change.

On windless days in September, broadwings may pass Hawk Mountain—but so far up they are literally out of sight.

As the high moves eastward, a southerly flow of air takes over in advance of the next front. Hawk activity may then increase, as birds use updrafts along the south slopes of the ridge. On days with southerly or easterly breezes, the South Lookout or a south-facing vantage point is best for hawk watching. After the September broadwing push, however, these winds seldom produce good flights.

To enjoy the spectacle of hawk migration at its dramatic best, one needs something in addition to favorable weather at the right location. One needs patience. Visitors cannot expect to arrive at a lookout for an hour and see thousands of hawks. Some first-time visitors do show up as a kettle of five hundred broadwings boils past or an eagle soars by just off the lookout.

Less lucky hawk-watchers have been coming to the sanctuary for years and are still waiting to see their first golden eagle or a really large kettle of broadwings.

It is more than pleasant just to sit quietly on a lookout on a spectacular fall day, hawks or no. But anyone fortunate enough to be on the mountain when the northwesterlies are blowing hawks down the sky and the lookout is astir with excitement will know the special magic of Hawk Mountain Sanctuary.

## Relative distribution of migrant raptors

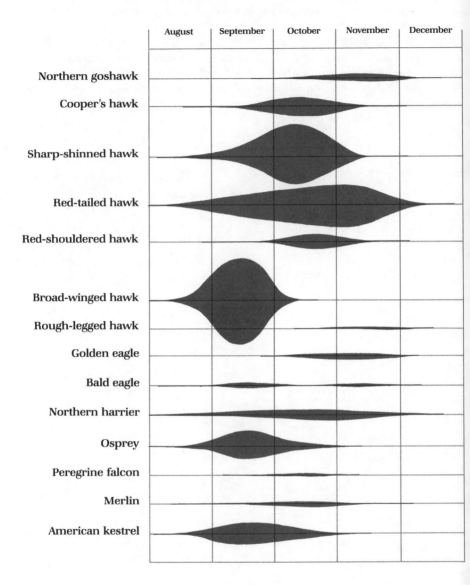

| | August | September | October | November | December |

Northern goshawk
Cooper's hawk
Sharp-shinned hawk
Red-tailed hawk
Red-shouldered hawk
Broad-winged hawk
Rough-legged hawk
Golden eagle
Bald eagle
Northern harrier
Osprey
Peregrine falcon
Merlin
American kestrel

Based on data collected at Hawk Mountain Sanctuary from 1934 to 1990. The chart does not include the turkey vulture or black vulture because theirs is not a true migration, but rather a southerly dispersal. The gyrfalcon and Swainson's hawk are not shown because they are very rarely seen at Hawk Mountain.

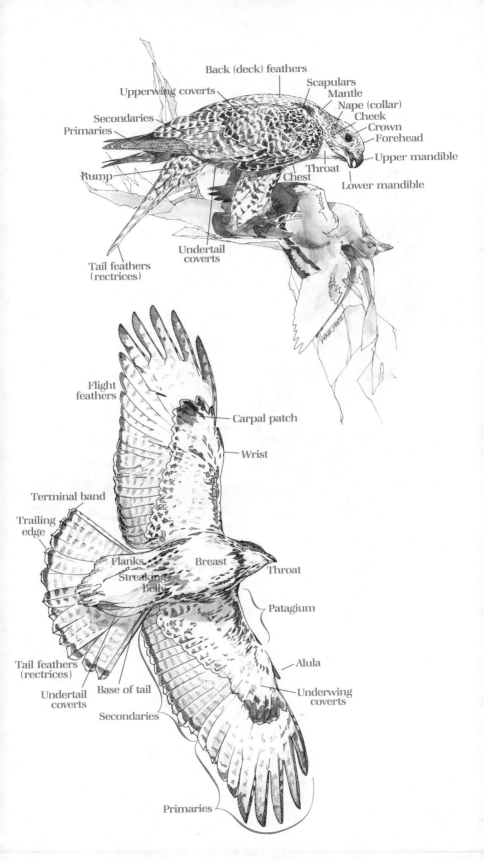

Back (deck) feathers

Upperwing coverts

Scapulars
Mantle
Nape (collar)
Cheek
Crown
Forehead

Secondaries

Primaries

Upper mandible

Throat

Rump

Chest

Lower mandible

Undertail
coverts

Tail feathers
(rectrices)

Flight
feathers

Carpal patch

Wrist

Terminal band

Trailing
edge

Flanks

Breast

Throat

Streaking
belly

Patagium

Alula

Tail feathers
(rectrices)

Underwing
coverts

Undertail
coverts

Base of tail

Secondaries

Primaries

# CHAPTER 5

# Hawks Aloft:
# Identifying the Raptors

This chapter contains information you will need to identify birds of prey in flight along northeastern ridges. Beginners, however, ought not expect to identify each passing hawk. This guide will enable you to narrow the field of choices, but remember that it takes many seasons of observation to become expert. Even then you will—or you should—record many birds as "unidents." The game of hawk watching is endlessly challenging.

Get to know which hawks are likely to appear during the time of your visit. Next, learn the basic shapes of these raptors (they're illustrated on the folding insert at the back of the book). If you are on the North Lookout, listen for the staff's identification. If you don't hear one of them call out the species, try to identify it yourself and then ask if you were correct. Staff members are here, in part, to help you become proficient in identification, but they will not call out the name of every passing bird.

You will notice that some people are able to identify raptors at great distances. Don't feel intimidated. Those folks have been coming to the lookouts for years and have learned the subtleties. Identification usually comes easily to them—but even the experts make mistakes. Identification of raptors on the wing requires quick assessment of several features: body shape and size, wing shape in relation to strength of the wind, and whether the bird is flapping, soaring, or gliding forward. Hawk-watchers refer to this kind of quick assessment as GISS (pronounced "jizz"), meaning general *i*mpression, *s*ize, and *s*hape. In most cases such an assessment will narrow the choice to the general type of raptor.

Accipiters (sharp-shinned hawk, Cooper's hawk, and northern goshawk) are small to medium in size, with short, rounded

*Hawks Aloft* is the title of Maurice Broun's book, the first written about Hawk Mountain Sanctuary. With respect and admiration this chapter is dedicated to his memory. His thirty-two-year curatorship ended with his retirement in 1966. He lived the remaining years of his life, until 1979, on a farm a few miles north of the sanctuary, within sight of the North Lookout.

## Taxonomy of the Raptors and Representative Silhouettes

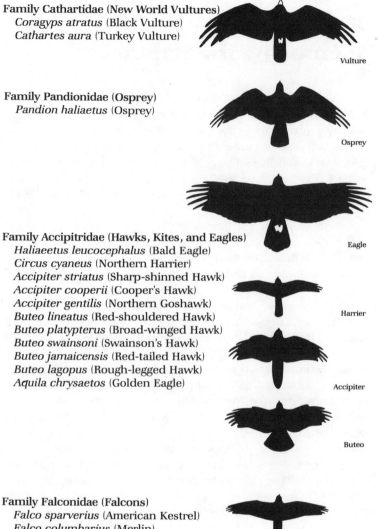

**Family Cathartidae (New World Vultures)**
 *Coragyps atratus* (Black Vulture)
 *Cathartes aura* (Turkey Vulture)

Vulture

**Family Pandionidae (Osprey)**
 *Pandion haliaetus* (Osprey)

Osprey

Eagle

**Family Accipitridae (Hawks, Kites, and Eagles)**
 *Haliaeetus leucocephalus* (Bald Eagle)
 *Circus cyaneus* (Northern Harrier)
 *Accipiter striatus* (Sharp-shinned Hawk)
 *Accipiter cooperii* (Cooper's Hawk)
 *Accipiter gentilis* (Northern Goshawk)
 *Buteo lineatus* (Red-shouldered Hawk)
 *Buteo platypterus* (Broad-winged Hawk)
 *Buteo swainsoni* (Swainson's Hawk)
 *Buteo jamaicensis* (Red-tailed Hawk)
 *Buteo lagopus* (Rough-legged Hawk)
 *Aquila chrysaetos* (Golden Eagle)

Harrier

Accipiter

Buteo

**Family Falconidae (Falcons)**
 *Falco sparverius* (American Kestrel)
 *Falco columbarius* (Merlin)
 *Falco peregrinus* (Peregrine Falcon)
 *Falco rusticolus* (Gyrfalcon)

Falcon

wings and long tails. This combination provides maneuverability when the bird is hunting and a characteristic flapping and gliding flight when migrating. Buteos (red-tailed hawk, red-shouldered hawk, broad-winged hawk, rough-legged hawk, and Swainson's hawk) are medium in size and have broad, flat wings and short, wide tails, which they use to catch rising air for soaring flight. Falcons (American kestrel, merlin, peregrine falcon, and gyrfalcon), small to medium in size, have long, pointed wings and long, narrow tails for fast flight.

The medium-sized northern harrier has a long tail and long wings that it holds in a dihedral. The larger osprey is also long-winged, but it holds its wings crooked at the wrist, giving a diagnostic M silhouette. Bald and golden eagles have long, flat wings and are the largest raptors that fly over Hawk Mountain.

Two species of vultures are also seen, the most common being the resident turkey vulture, a large, dark bird that holds up its wings in a diagnostic V. The rarer black vulture has flat, rounded wings and a very short tail. Neither of these birds has feathers on its head.

## Noonday Lulls

Hawk-watchers at the lookouts have found that some species tend to be less active at certain times of day than at others. One of the most curious phenomena is the noonday lull—a scarcity of migrants at midday. Although there is no generally accepted explanation for such a lull, two common hypotheses center on thermal dynamics and hunting. Noonday lulls are common during broadwing season in September. Thermal activity is then at its peak, and thermal activity is greatest during midday. It may simply be that broadwings (and other hawks) are being lofted beyond the range of binoculars and that vision is reduced at the same time by atmospheric conditions. Perhaps, too, other species—the sharp-shinned hawk, for example—spend the midday hours resting or hunting in the forest below the lookouts.

## Points of Reference

The panorama from the North Lookout reproduced on the folding insert shows common points of reference and distances from the lookout. The most frequently used reference points are nos. 1–5 because hawks are typically first spotted as they appear at one of these points—either over, under, or next to it. The points were named by Maurice Broun in 1934 during his first season on the North Lookout as the official counter.

Identifying birds overhead can be tricky. Your perception is affected not only by the bird's distance from the lookout but also by the conditions of the sky. Birds are much easier to spot in cloudy skies than in clear ones: hawks get lost in bright blue, cloudless skies. Furthermore, their altitude above the lookout is sometimes difficult to determine and so, consequently, is their size. Your perception of a bird's linear and altitudinal distance is influenced by the quality of optics you use.

## Tools of the Trade

Binoculars are absolutely essential if you want to identify migrants and see plumage details. Hawks on migration can be enjoyed with the naked eye, but optics reveal a whole new dimension.

Binoculars range in price from $20 or so to $1,000 or more. The cheaper the model, however, the greater the potential for problems. Inexpensive "sporting" binoculars tend to become misaligned and usually are not worth repairing. Many hawk-

watchers use medium-priced glasses ($150–$200) and get years of good use from them.

A great variety of styles and powers of magnification is available. Generally speaking, the best power for hawk watching is 8× or 10×, but a 7× general birding binocular will serve quite satisfactorily.

Spotting scopes are used by serious birders. While binoculars seldom exceed 15× magnification, spotting scopes typically provide 20× or 30×, even 60×. Often binoculars and spotting scopes are used alternately, the selection depending on the situation. A scope can be mounted either on a tripod—a hindrance on a rocky vantage point such as the North Lookout—or on a gunstock.

The staff of Hawk Mountain Sanctuary are experienced in the use and care of binoculars and scopes. Feel free to ask them questions.

## Clothing and Food

It is important to dress appropriately for hawk watching on the lookouts. Fall days can be sunny, with temperatures in the 90s, or there can be snow, 50-mile-per-hour winds, and a wind-chill factor of −30. The North Lookout is typically 10 degrees cooler than the valley.

Years of experience by Hawk Mountain staff have shown that several layers of clothing work better than any single garment because layers can be removed or added as the weather dictates. A light down jacket over a wool sweater is often adequate. A heavy down jacket is advisable for the blustery days of November and December, but again in conjunction with layers of wool. A long stay on the lookout is also made more comfortable by a foam pad or cushion or a small carpet remnant to sit on.

Food cannot be purchased at the sanctuary, and the nearest markets are ten miles away in the villages of Wanamakers (northeast on Pennsylvania Route 143), Lenhartsville (southeast on Route 143), and Orwigsburg (northwest off Route 61). Restaurants are located along the major roads to the mountain.

Eating is the favorite pastime of some hawk-watchers; for them, lunch can span the day. Insulated containers for hot or cold drinks or soup are desirable. Dehydration can be a problem during the hot days of September, and hypothermia must be guarded against in November and December, especially if you spend the entire day on the North Lookout.

The species descriptions are presented in an order that facilitates comparative identification, not taxonomic order. Included with each are lookout tips, which are designed to be used on the North Lookout.

## Turkey Vulture                                    VULTURE

*Cathartes aura*

**Overall Impression:** A large (eagle-sized), dark bird with a small head and a long tail.
**In Flight:** Wings are held in a strong V, or dihedral. A slow-motion dip of the wings to adjust flight is common. Rocking flight is diagnostic. Occasionally flaps with deep wingbeats.

**Position View**
**1a. Above:** Dark brown throughout except adult has red, featherless head, and immature's head is gray and featherless.
**1b. Below:** Primary and secondary feathers metallic gray, otherwise dark brown throughout.
**1c. Head On:** Long wings held in a strong dihedral. Much rocking.
**1d. Full Display:** Strongly angled wing on a glide. Primary and secondary feathers appear metallic gray below, but dark above.
**1e. Profile:** Strong dihedral of wings is evident.

## Black Vulture                                     VULTURE

*Coragyps atratus*

**Overall Impression:** A large, dark bird with broad, plank-shaped wings. At a distance appears to be a "flying wing."
**In Flight:** Steady flight without rocking. A series of quick wingbeats followed by a flat-winged soar. No dihedral.

**Position View**
**2a. Above:** Dark brown to black throughout except for prominent white patches near wingtips. Head dark gray and featherless.
**2b. Below:** Dark brown to black throughout except for prominent white patches near wingtips. White patches more prominent when viewed from below.
**2c. Head On:** Wings held flat or with a very slight dihedral.

**Could Be Confused With**
Turkey vultures and black vultures are most often confused with bald eagles and golden eagles. The constant rocking flight of TVs and the flying-wing appearance of BVs should remove any doubt.

**Lookout Tips**
Turkey vultures are seen from late February through mid-November. They constantly tack back and forth past the lookout. Often a kettle of turkey vultures can be sighted off no. 1 on the far horizon and can be mistaken for broadwings.
Black vultures are usually observed flying together, not singly as turkey vultures often do. Black vultures are commonly seen between the Kittatinny Ridge and the Pinnacle, rarely north of the ridge, and often at great distances out over the valley.

Fred Wetzel, a former member of the Hawk Mountain staff and a professional bird artist, executed the raptor plates.

Turkey Vulture

Black Vulture

1a

2a

1b

2b

2c

1c

1d

1e

Bald Eagle

Golden Eagle

*Haliaeetus leucocephalus*

**Overall Impression:** A massive, flat-winged bird of prey with an out-sized beak, long head and neck, and comparatively short tail.

**In Flight:** Recognized at a distance by the large body suspended under long, wide, flat wings. Flap is slow and ponderous. Wings are held well above the plane of the body of a glide. Trailing edge of wing is straight.

## Position View

**a.** Above, Adult: Very dark brown except for snow white head and tail. Large yellow beak obvious at close range. Wings wide throughout length.

**b.** Above, Subadult: Dark with highly variable white mottling throughout. Head and tail may show some white, depending on age. Buffy eye line. Heavily mottled pale triangle behind neck. Full adult plumage is attained at four to six years of age.

**c.** Above, Immature: First- and second-year birds dark brown throughout with some mottling.

**d.** Below, Adult: Dark body and wings. White head and tail.

**e.** Below, Subadult: Neck and upper breast brown with some mottling. Lower breast and belly white with brown flecking. Tail variably mottled.

**f.** Below, Immature: Body brown throughout. Underwing lining whitish from body to primaries.

**g.** Profile: Wide wings angled slightly forward on a set glide.

**h.** Head On: White head of adult dramatically visible (headlight-like). Wings held level or elevated above horizontal plane. Low-slung body.

**i.** Full Display: Very prominent white head and tail.

**j.** Tuck.

## Could Be Confused With

**Golden Eagle:** Wings may be held in a slight dihedral. Head and beak smaller; longer tail appears thicker at base than at tip. Trailing edge slightly S-curved. Immature's broad white underwing patches and white basal area on tail concentrated, not diffuse.

**Osprey:** Underside white throughout. Prominently crooked wing narrower than the bald eagle's.

**Turkey Vulture:** Black throughout except for metallic gray primaries and secondaries. Wings held in a strong dihedral.

**Black Vulture** (not illustrated): Very small head and short tail. Flaps are quick and shallow rather than slow and deep.

## Lookout Tips

Bald Eagles occasionally fly with their wings in a slight dihedral. They may be seen at any altitude and coming from any direction. They are best viewed on a northwest wind, when they come close to the north side of the lookout. Sightings are on the rise now that re-introduction programs are under way in many eastern states.

adult

subadult

immature

Golden Eagle

Osprey

Turkey Vulture

# Golden Eagle

*Aquila chrysaetos*

**Overall Impression:** A massive bird of prey that could be likened to an oversized buteo. Very long, broad wings, chunky body, and a broad, thick tail.

**In Flight:** Wings constricted at base, resulting in a slightly S-curved trailing edge, especially when gliding. Flaps are deep and labored, but wings are rarely raised above the body plane. Exhibits a slight dihedral on a glide.

## Position View

The tail feathers of golden eagles molt gradually over a long period. At any one time there may be several generations of feathers on the same tail. Tails show varying degrees of white until the birds reach age seven, by which time they are all dark.

**a. Above, Adult:** Dark throughout, sometimes with dingy mottling. Small white area occasionally visible on either side of tail. Golden hackles observable at close range.

**b. Above, Subadult:** Dark brown. Upper half of tail white.

**c. Above, Immature:** Very dark brown with prominent white patches at bases of primaries. Upper two-thirds of tail white.

**d. Below, Adult:** Dark throughout, although some individuals show dark brown mixed with lighter brown on secondaries and primaries.

**e. Below, Subadult:** Basically dark brown. Conspicuous white patches at bases of primaries. White at base of tail sometimes mottled with brown.

**f. Below, Immature:** Dark brown body. Large, concentrated white patches on wings at the bases of four primaries and about six secondaries. Tail mostly white, with broad dark terminal band.

**g. Head On:** Long wings held in a slight dihedral, never as pronounced as a turkey vulture's. At this angle, wings on the downstroke nearly wrap around the body.

**h. Tuck:** On a glide at or above eye level, wings are strongly angled back. On strong winds, primaries are held together.

## Could Be Confused With

**Bald Eagle (Immature):** Bald eagles have a long head (accentuated by massive beak) and shorter tail. They flap more and soar less than golden eagles.

**Northern Harrier:** At a distance, the white rump of the harrier could be mistaken for the white basal tail feathers of the golden eagle, but the harrier's size and proportions are quite different.

**Rough-legged Hawk:** A smaller version of the golden eagle. Wings are narrower, and the light and normal morphs have prominent dark patches on the light underwing.

**Turkey Vulture:** Possible confusion at a distance, but look for the vulture's rocking and strong dihedral. Eagles soar on flat or slightly upheld wings and never rock.

## Lookout Tips

Golden eagles normally fly late in the day. They confidently soar on blustery northwest winds, a mark of their massive size. Typically they appear above no. 4 or no. 5 and glide with set wings close to the north side of the ridge. On light winds golden eagles are frequently seen off the distant south-facing slope of no. 1; they avoid the North Lookout by flying out across the valley toward the Pinnacle.

a

b

c

adult

subadult

immature

d

e

f

h

g

Bald
Eagle
(imm.)

Northern
Harrier

Rough-legged
Hawk

Turkey
Vulture

# Sharp-shinned Hawk ACCIPITER

*Accipiter striatus*

**Overall Impression:** A slender, agile, bluejay-sized hawk with short, rounded wings and a long, usually notched square tail.

**In Flight:** Easily buffeted by wind; erratic flight line. A rapid flutter of somewhat stiff, shallow wingbeats followed by a glide, repeated often. Like all accipiters (and some other hawks) a flap-flap-flap—glide. Wings held forward. Tail twists, as if ruddering, when wind shifts.

## Position View

**a. Above, Adult:** Blue-gray to slate with slightly darker cap. Three to five straight dark bands apparent on tail at close range. Conspicuous white undertail coverts.

**b. Above, Immature:** Brown back with light feather edges. Darker bands of tail and of trailing edge of wing less conspicuous than in adult. White undertail coverts less noticeable.

**c. Below, Adult:** Small head. Body constricts at base of tail. Rusty barring on breast and belly. Undertail coverts white. Axillaries tawny to rusty.

**d. Below, Immature:** Shape like that of adult but very dense brown to rusty streaking on breast and belly, with no apparent pattern.

**e. Profile:** Body mass concentrated toward head. Small head appears tucked between leading edge of each wing. Tail usually tilts above horizontal plane. (Cooper's hawk appears elongated and broad-shouldered. Holds body even to horizontal; occasionally lifts head and neck above horizontal. Larger head. More mass to white undertail coverts.)

**f. Head On:** Compact cross section. Wings tip down but rarely extend below body.

**g. Full Display:** Tail can be fanned out. Wings reach forward, highlighting "pinched hip" at base of tail. Tail and trailing edge of wing with noticeable banding. Trailing edge of wing angled forward slightly from body to tip.

**h. Tuck:** Wings pulled into body, especially in moderate and gusting wind; sometimes appear pointed. Tail extends beyond wingtips, unlike in falcons.

## Could Be Confused With

**Cooper's Hawk:** Elongated. Big head. Longer, rounded tail; white terminal band often more prominent in adult. Steadier flight.

**American Kestrel:** Long, pointed, sickle-shaped wings that, in tuck position, extend to end of tail. Dark moustache apparent at close range. Deeper, less stiff wingbeat.

**Broad-winged Hawk:** Wide, broad wings with sharper angle at wrist. When broadwing glides on a thermal, wingtip appears slightly more pointed and massive. Proportionately shorter, broader tail.

**Merlin:** Larger head. Heavily streaked underparts. Tail with wide dark bands. Powerful, steady, rowing flight. In tuck, wingtips extend to tip of tail.

## Lookout Tips

The smallest, quickest accipiters, sharpshins (sharpies) have a jittery flight behavior. They frequently attack the owl decoy hanging at the North Lookout and often harass other hawks. Their numbers increase in late September and usually peak before mid-October. Sharpies hunt around the North Lookout in the early morning and are often the first hawks to be seen.

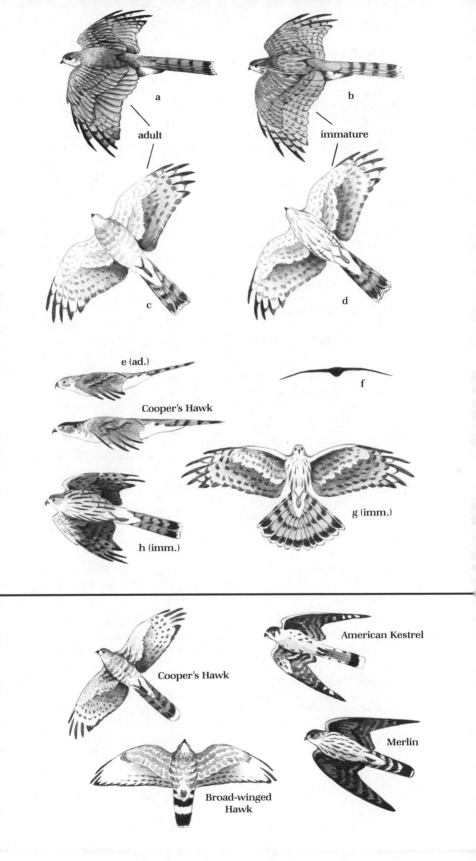

a

adult

b

immature

c

d

e (ad.)

Cooper's Hawk

f

h (imm.)

g (imm.)

Cooper's Hawk

American Kestrel

Broad-winged
Hawk

Merlin

*Accipiter cooperii*

**Overall Impression:** A slender, crow-sized hawk. Larger version of the sharp-shinned hawk. Flimsy, loose tail as long as body and usually rounded.

**In Flight:** Steady, sustained flight, unlike erratic flight of sharpshin. Flap is from the shoulder, not the wrist, making it seem more rigid. Less flapping (although more powerful) and more sailing than sharpshin: flap-flap-flap—g—l—i—d—e, as opposed to flap-flap-flap—glide of sharpshin. Head protrudes beyond leading edge of wing.

## Position View

**a. Above, Adult:** Bluish to slate back. Strong color contrast between back and crown. White undertail coverts appear to wrap up to and partially around base of rump. Pronounced white terminal tail band.

**b. Above, Immature:** Brown back. Dark bands on tail more conspicuous at close range. White terminal tail band often twice the width of sharpshin's and brighter.

**c. Below, Adult:** Richer rusty coloration on breast compared with sharpshin. Tail long and usually rounded.

**d. Below, Immature:** Breast streaking is finer than on sharpshin. Overall light or creamy appearance, especially toward flanks.

**e. Profile:** Head protrudes well beyond wing line, as opposed to the often tucked appearance of sharpshin's head. When viewed at eye level or slightly above, head can appear to stretch upward as if bird is looking around. White undertail coverts conspicuous.

**f. Head On:** Proportionately larger neck and head than smaller sharpshin. Wings less downcurved.

**g. Full Display:** Terminal band conspicuous when tail is fanned. Tail long, wings straight and relatively short.

**h. Tuck:** Wings swept back when sailing on moderate to stiff winds but extend no farther than flanks. White undertail coverts pronounced and tail usually rounded.

## Could Be Confused With

**Northern Goshawk (immature):** Broad and heavy. Tail not as rounded and can appear wedge-shaped. Broad tail and proportionately shorter wings give stubby appearance. Flap continuous and powerful.

**Sharp-shinned Hawk:** Smaller version of Cooper's. Head tucked into "shoulders." Tail usually square and sometimes notched. Has longer wings compared with body size than does Cooper's or goshawk. Flight erratic and nervous.

**Red-shouldered Hawk (immature):** The most slender and narrow-winged of the buteos. Translucent crescents—"windows"—at wingtips. Flight buoyant and light (butterfly-like). Flap loose and weak. Sails and circles more than Cooper's.

## Lookout Tips

Sharp-shinned and Cooper's hawks migrate together; but Cooper's hawks move throughout October (immatures migrate before adults), whereas sharpies peak in early October. At Hawk Mountain, as at most eastern ridgetops, the ratio of Cooper's hawks to sharpshins is about 1:16. Cooper's hawks are seen mostly north of the North Lookout.

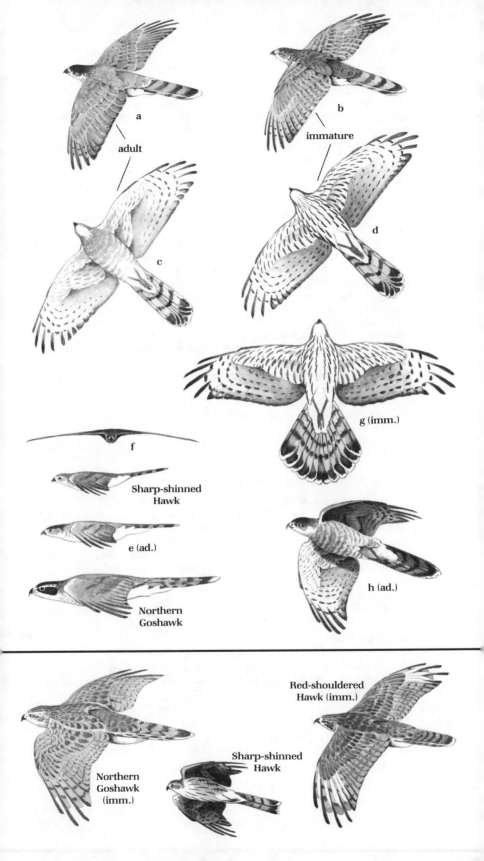

a

b

adult

immature

c

d

g (imm.)

f

Sharp-shinned
Hawk

e (ad.)

Northern
Goshawk

h (ad.)

Northern
Goshawk
(imm.)

Sharp-shinned
Hawk

Red-shouldered
Hawk (imm.)

# Northern Goshawk

*Accipiter gentilis*

**Overall Impression:** The largest of the three accipiters seen at Hawk Mountain; has as much body mass as a buteo. Moderately rounded, long tail that sometimes appears wedge-shaped. Because of its thick body, the tail can appear short compared with that of Cooper's.
**In Flight:** Steady, determined flight with deep, powerful wingbeats. Stable in strong winds.

## Position View

**a. Above, Adult:** Slate gray back. Tail bands wavy, unlike straight bands on sharpshin and Cooper's. Head with dark cap, prominent white eye line, and dark cheek patch. Undertail coverts large, strikingly white, and fluffy.

**b. Above, Immature:** Back appears mottled and decidedly more honey-colored than that of Cooper's. Tail bands dark and wavy. Face dull brown with tan-to-white eye line that can be difficult to recognize in flying bird. Undertail coverts prominent but brown-streaked.

**c. Below, Adult:** Breast appears silvery gray (white with gray barring). Lower wing surface uniform in appearance. Conspicuous fluffy white undertail coverts. Large chest. Tail appears short compared with rest of body and has small terminal band.

**d. Below, Immature:** Dense brown breast streaking. Streaked undertail coverts.

**e. Profile:** Buteo-like in appearance. Prominent thickness to base of wings and tail.

**f. Head On:** Body appears to hang from wings because of heavy chest. Wingtips extend below body when gliding. Wings thick in shoulder area.

**g. Full Display:** Broad and relatively short wings contrast with heavy body. Broad-based tail rarely fans.

**h. Tuck:** On a swift glide, wings are held back and pointed. Massiveness is quite evident in the tuck position.

## Could Be Confused With

**Red-shouldered Hawk (immature):** Redshoulder sails and circles; goshawk rarely does either. Flight of redshoulder is loose and floppy compared with determined flight of goshawk.

**Cooper's Hawk:** Easily confused with immature goshawk. Body slender with flimsy, loose tail. Acceleration more agile or loose compared with strong goshawk flight. Goshawk is wide; Cooper's hawk is long.

**Red-tailed Hawk (immature):** Wings broader, tail shorter. Breast white to creamy, not silvery or streaked.

## Lookout Tips

Goshawks, undaunted by stiff winds, seem to favor the rawest and most blustery of November days. Sharpshins hug the ridge; Cooper's hawks tend to veer off to the north, avoiding the lookout; goshawks fly above eye level and almost always fly north of the ridge.

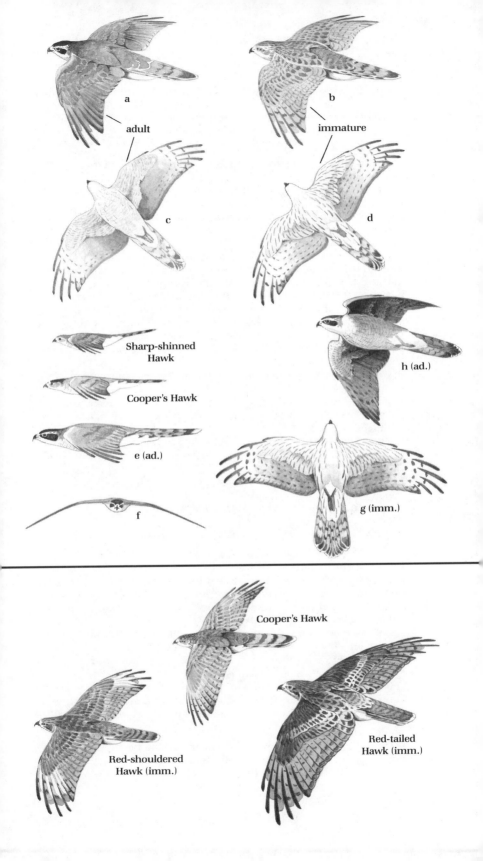

adult

immature

c

d

Sharp-shinned
Hawk

Cooper's Hawk

e (ad.)

f

h (ad.)

g (imm.)

Cooper's Hawk

Red-shouldered
Hawk (imm.)

Red-tailed
Hawk (imm.)

# Red-tailed Hawk BUTEO

*Buteo jamaicensis*

**Overall Impression:** A robust hawk with broad, rounded wings and short tail.

**In Flight:** When soaring, redtail moves in wide circles and flaps little. Often glides, sometimes with a slight dihedral.

## Position View

Both adult and immature redtails are highly variable in their plumage, mostly in the belly band area. Although a belly band, carpal patches, and patagial markings are usually evident, redtails are more susceptible to albinism than other hawks.

**a. Above, Adult:** Back variably brown and mottled. Rusty or rufous tail color varies in richness and hue. Undertail coverts can give impression of white rump.

**b. Above, Immature:** Overall plumage resembles adult's, but more mottled. Tail gray-brown with narrow dark bands. Fluffy white undertail coverts can give impression of white rump.

**c. Below, Adult:** White with random streaking on midbreast, commonly referred to as the "belly band." Belly band streaking variable and occasionally hard to see. Undertail a washed-out version of the more rusty dorsal side. Primaries tipped with black. Prominent dark patagium, or epaulet, on leading edge of wing. Prominent crescent-shaped carpal (wrist) patch.

**d. Below, Immature:** Resembles adult in overall appearance. Tail light brown with fine barring.

**e. Profile:** Large soaring hawk with heavy chest. Wingtips held up in glide or soar. Belly band appears as random brown streaking from midbreast to flanks.

**f. Head On:** Heavy chest prominent. Large, rounded wings thick toward base. Leading edges of wings near body white, commonly called "headlights."

**g. Full Display:** Soaring or circling in thermals: wingtips up, primaries spread wide, tail fanned. Gliding: Wings held level or slightly downward with tips up. Plumages highly variable, but belly band is most diagnostic feature.

**h. Tuck:** Wings wide throughout. Wingtips appear black when primaries compressed.

## Could Be Confused With

**Red-shouldered Hawk (immature):** Redshoulder's soaring circle is tighter and boxlike, whereas redtail's is wide and circular. Flap of redshoulder is loose and relaxed; redtail's wingbeats are deep and labored. No belly band in redshoulder.

**Golden Eagle (immature):** Confused at a distance with redtail. Prominent white feathers at base of tail and white wing patches. Massive body hangs from wide wings held horizontal. Takes much longer to complete a circle; flap is labored.

**Rough-legged Hawk (light morph):** Wide, variably streaked belly band. Dark carpal patches. Soars or glides with a more pronounced dihedral. Redtails outnumber roughlegs at Hawk Mountain by 1,000:1.

## Lookout Tips

During early fall resident redtails can usually be sighted on the north slope, often hovering above the forest in search of prey. Redtails typically migrate late in the day and can be seen until sunset.

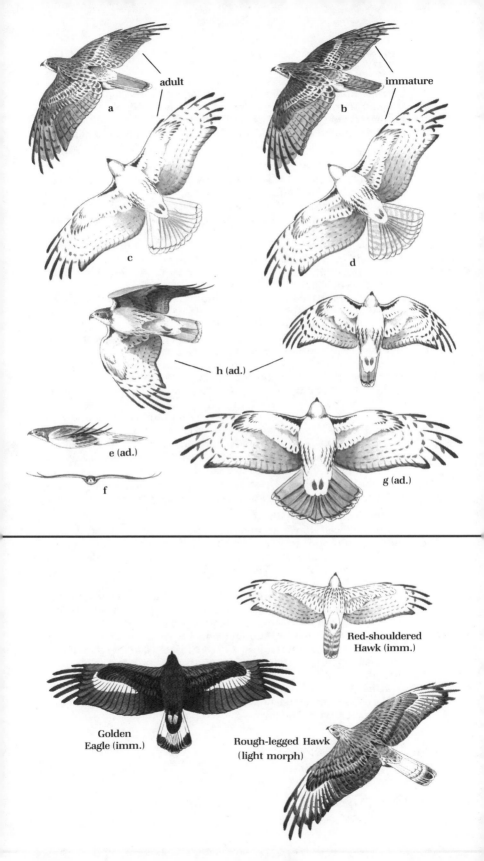

adult

immature

a

b

c

d

h (ad.)

e (ad.)

f

g (ad.)

Red-shouldered Hawk (imm.)

Golden Eagle (imm.)

Rough-legged Hawk (light morph)

# Red-shouldered Hawk BUTEO

*Buteo lineatus*

**Overall Impression:** A slim buteo with long, narrow wings and a long tail. Body narrow compared with robust body of redtail.

**In Flight:** A delicate soaring bird with loose, shallow, butterfly-like wingbeats. Often a few rapid wingbeats followed by a short glide.

## Position View

**a.** **Above, Adult:** Rich brown body with rufous or rusty shoulder patches. Tail long and black with three distinct narrow white bands and white tip. Translucent crescent-shaped areas ("windows") at bases of primaries visible, but more so from underside. (Light areas at the bases of primaries can be evident in other hawks but are rarely crescent-shaped.)

**b.** **Above, Immature:** Brown body with variable mottling. Wings gray-brown and mottled. Tail banding less distinct than in adult. Windows visible on a soar, more so from underside. Rufous shoulder often indistinguishable.

**c.** **Below, Adult:** Rich rufous underplumage. Striking reddish shoulders. White to buff translucent windows at bases of primaries. Tail black with three narrow white bands.

**d.** **Below, Immature:** Dull white body with dark brown chest streaking. Little rufous in wing lining or shoulders. Windows visible but not as pronounced as in adult. Tail banding indistinct unless tail spread while soaring, even then difficult to see.

**e.** **Head On:** Long wings narrow at base and can appear pointed. Slender chest.

**f. Full Display:** Body tube-shaped. When redshoulder soars in a thermal, wings are relatively longer than broadwing's or redtail's. Tail is spread and shows prominent banding in adult, less in immature. Depending on the lighting some rufous is visible in immature, but very conspicuous in adult under any lighting.

**g.** **Tuck:** Slender body. Heavy upper breast streaking on immature; fine barring on adult. Tail broad. Wings reach forward on a glide.

## Could Be Confused With

**Broad-winged Hawk (immature):** More squat, broader. Barrel-chested. No prominent crescent wing windows. Much wider subterminal tail band. Flap is direct and from the shoulder; redshoulder flaps more from the wrist. The broadwing migration is usually over by the time redshoulders arrive.

**Cooper's Hawk:** Redshoulders can resemble accipters in flight, but they do much more circling and soaring. Both species fan their tails, but the relatively longer wings, narrow white tail bands, and wing windows of redshoulders should distinguish the two.

**Red-tailed Hawk (immature):** Breast streaking confined to midsection (belly band); streaking in immature redshoulder is darker on chest than flanks.

**Goshawk (not illustrated):** When viewed overhead, immature goshawks can resemble redshoulders. The chest of the goshawk is heavier compared with the narrow-chested redshoulder.

## Lookout Tips

Red-shouldered hawks tend to appear off no. 1 and fly across the Kettle.

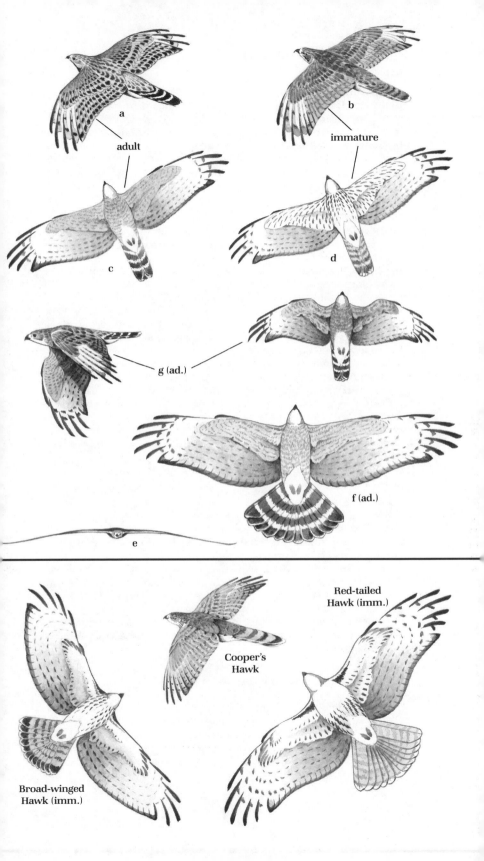

a

adult

b

immature

c

d

g (ad.)

f (ad.)

e

Red-tailed Hawk (imm.)

Cooper's Hawk

Broad-winged Hawk (imm.)

*Buteo platypterus*

**Overall Impression:** A smaller version of the red-tailed hawk. Body plump and barrel-chested. Tail stubby. Wings broad and relatively short; appear to taper on a glide.

**In Flight:** A master of soaring. Wide wings and fanned tail allow broadwings to take full advantage of lift from thermal air currents. Will break out of the very top of the thermal and stream, either in single file or on a broad front, to the next rising air pocket. Flap is stiff on flat wings and often rapid. On a glide, wings have curved leading edges and straight trailing edges.

### Position View

**a. Above, Adult:** Uniformly brown and drab except for highly visible broad alternating black-and-white tail bands. Terminal black tail band wider than others.

**b. Above, Immature:** Same drab uniformity as adult. Tail marking indistinct except for the terminal band, which is narrower than the more conspicuous terminal tail band of adult.

**c. Below, Adult:** Breast buff-colored with fine cinnamon barring. Concentration of brown streaks sometimes gives a belly band appearance. Underwings white with dark fringe from secondaries around to trailing edge. Wing lining lightly buff-colored.

**d. Below, Immature:** White breast with brown streaking. Underwings pale white. Gaps left by molting primaries often mistaken for "windows." Leading and trailing wing edges with dark border. Tail bands indistinct except for terminal band, which is often visible when tail is fanned.

**e. Head On:** Wings flat and held at right angles to body. Very tips may turn slightly upward. Light forehead gives "headlight" appearance. Tail may twist slightly from side to side (ruddering).

**f. Full Display:** Same characteristics as for Adult, Below.

**g. Tuck.**

### Could Be Confused With

**Red-shouldered Hawk (immature):** Sleek body with longer, narrow wings. Folded tail is broad-based and wider throughout than narrow closed tail of broadwing. Flap loose and butterfly-like, unlike stiff, choppy flap of broadwing.

**Sharp-shinned Hawk:** Broadwings on a high glide can resemble sharpshins because of the narrow tail configuration, reminiscent of an accipiter, but sharpshins are much smaller and have short, rounded wings and longer, narrower tails.

**Red-tailed Hawk (not illustrated):** Rarely migrates in September. Those that are seen are usually local birds remaining near summer breeding grounds.

### Lookout Tips

Look for broad-winged hawks rising from the forest on September mornings when the sun begins to create thermal updrafts. During productive days kettles of broadwings can appear as far-off swarms on all horizons. Typically, broadwings move in great numbers down across the Appalachian ridge system a day or two after the passage of a cold front. Development of a large kettle is largely dependent on the weather. Call the sanctuary (215-756-6961) anytime during the migration for general flight information.

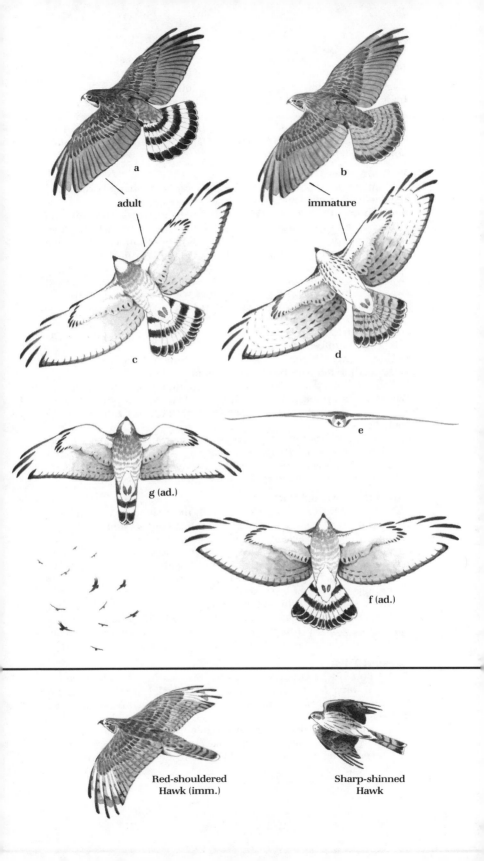

adult

immature

a

b

c

d

e

g (ad.)

f (ad.)

Red-shouldered
Hawk (imm.)

Sharp-shinned
Hawk

# Rough-legged Hawk BUTEO

*Buteo lagopus*

**Overall Impression:** A large buteo with long wings, long tail, slender body, short neck, small head, and small bill. A miniature of the golden eagle.

**In Flight:** Wings held slightly above body plane in a modified dihedral, suggesting Northern Harrier. Flap is slow and easy, and often appears to be double-jointed.

## Position View

Plumages are extremely variable; general body shape is the more reliable field mark. Adults and immatures are similar.

**a–c. Above, All Color Morphs:** Long, narrow wings and tail. Tail white; male's tail multibanded, with broad black terminal tail band; female's tail not multibanded, but with broad terminal band. Immature dark morph can have an all-black tail. White rump may be evident. Short neck; small, rounded head.

**d. Below, Light Morph:** Breast white with wide belly band. Carpal (wrist) patches apparent. Dark primaries with dark border on trailing edge of wing. Broad terminal tail band.

**e. Below, Normal (or Intermediate) Morph:** Upper breast streaked with brown; lower breast uniformly brown. Dark carpal patches. Terminal tail band brown.

**f. Below, Dark Morph:** Underbody dark brown. Underwing coverts brown. White tail with broad dark terminal tail band.

**g. Head On:** Wing raised in a modified dihedral. Much wrist action on wingbeat, as opposed to stiff wingbeat of redtail and golden eagle. Light leading edge of wing especially noticeable in lighter plumage morphs.

**h. Soaring:** Wings held in a modified dihedral and positioned forward. Swainson's hawks, northern harriers, red-tailed hawks, golden eagles, and turkey vultures all exhibit degrees of the dihedral. Check other field marks to confirm identification of the roughleg.

## Could Be Confused With

**Northern Harrier:** Wings narrow, body more slender. A much more dainty bird. Tail dark; very prominent white rump. Wings held with stronger dihedral. Tacks constantly when gliding.

**Golden Eagle:** A massive bird with long, wide wings, broader tail, and larger head. Wingbeat is deep and labored. On a glide, golden eagles have relatively flat wings with wingtips down. At times a slight dihedral is exhibited.

**Turkey Vulture:** Dihedral more pronounced. Rarely flaps, but rocks constantly. Smaller head and shorter tail. Common throughout fall season, whereas roughlegs are rare. Turkey vultures have usually moved south before roughlegs arrive.

## Lookout Tips

The Rough-legged hawk is the rarest regularly occurring migrant raptor at Hawk Mountain. Individuals are usually seen in November. In some years only four or five are recorded, while in others there may be twelve or more.

The roughleg is also the most variable in plumage, ranging from light morphs to almost completely black ones, and every combination in between. Flight attitude may be a more definitive identification characteristic.

a

light
morph

b

normal
morph

c

dark
morph

d

e

f

g

h

Turkey
Vulture

Northern
Harrier

Golden
Eagle

*Buteo swainsoni*

**Overall Impression:** A redtail-sized buteo with long, narrow, pointed wings.

**In Flight:** Like other buteos, utilizes thermal air currents. Wings often held in a dihedral; can be confused with northern harrier.

## Position View

Swainson's hawks are rare visitors to the Northeast. They occur singly or in kettles of broad-winged hawks. Plumages are highly variable, and there is little difference between adults and immatures.

**a. Below, Light Morph:** Chestnut-colored neck band separates white belly from white throat patch. Flight feathers and underwing coverts light with prominent dark tips. Tail grayish, ending with wide subterminal band.

**b. Below, Dark Morph:** Sooty throughout. Underwing feathers marked with black.

**c. Head On:** Long, narrow wings held in a dihedral.

**d. Soaring:** Reminiscent of a harrier, with wings in a dihedral and teetering or rocking flight. In light phase, light underwing feathers show prominently when wings held in a dihedral.

## Could Be Confused With

**Red-tailed Hawk:** Approximately the same size, but wings broader and less pointed.

**Broad-winged Hawk:** Smaller, with shorter wings. Underbody and underwing coloration quite different.

**Northern Harrier** (not illustrated): Same flight style, but body slenderer, wings narrower. Prominent white rump.

## Lookout Tips

Swainson's hawks appear during the broadwing season of mid-September. Their occurrence is rare; but perhaps because the broadwings have not been scrutinized carefully enough, Swainson's hawks may have been undercounted.

a

b

c

d

Red-tailed Hawk

Broad-winged Hawk

# American Kestrel

*Falco sparverius*

**Overall Impression:** A small (robin-sized) raptor with slender, sickle-shaped wings. The smallest and most common falcon seen at Hawk Mountain.

**In Flight:** Buoyant and graceful on the wing, kestrels fly with rapid, rowing wingbeats. Their flight is not direct, and they tend to flap then dart as they move past the lookout. Kestrels also occur in kettles with broad-winged hawks.

## Position View

**a. Above, Adult Male:** Black rufous, wings blue-gray. Top of head slate-colored with rufous crown patch, not easily seen in flight. Primary feathers black and spotted on inner margin. Rufous tail with wide black terminal tail band tipped in white. Dark moustache and very white cheek patch visible when bird tilts.

**b. Above, Adult Female:** Back and wings rufous with black barring. Lacks the brightness of the male. A less vivid moustache visible as the bird tilts. Paler tail narrowly banded; subterminal tail band wider than other bands, but not as wide as male's.

**Above, Immature** (not illustrated): Same as adult male or female.

**c. Below, Adult Male:** Buff to rufous breast. Prominent black spots on flanks and outer tail feathers.

**d. Below, Adult Female:** Buff to cream breast with darker buff to rufous streaking.

**Below, Immature** (not illustrated): Both sexes resemble adult female.

**e. Head On:** Long, slender wings. Moustache usually evident.

**f. Full Display:** Soars with tail fanned in light wind. Sexual dimorphism (male and female plumage differences) clearly evident in this position.

**g. Tuck:** Long, pointed wings pulled toward flanks on moderate to brisk winds.

## Could Be Confused With

**Sharp-shinned Hawk:** Wings broader and rounder. In a tuck, primaries short compared with those of kestrel. In a soar, sharpshin is square-tailed, kestrel round-tailed.

**Merlin:** Body heavier. Plumage darker. Lacks prominent moustache. Wings broader, thicker. Flies with strong and determined flaps, unlike flapping-darting flight of kestrel.

## Lookout Tips

Kestrels, the earliest migrant raptors, begin to move in early August. They are often seen snatching and eating dragonflies or migrating monarch butterflies.

adult
male

adult
female

a

b

c

d

f (♂)

g (♂)

e

Sharp-shinned
Hawk

Merlin

# Merlin FALCON

*Falco columbarius*

**Overall Impression:** A dark, pigeon-sized falcon with broad-based, long, sickle-shaped wings whose "hands" are much longer than the "forearms."

**In Flight:** Strong and determined. Seldom soars or glides; appears always to be in a hurry.

**Position View**

**a. Above, Adult Male:** Bluish gray back. Tail with wide dark bands.

**b. Above, Adult Female:** Dark brown throughout. Tail like male's, but brown.

**Above, Immature** (not illustrated): Resembles adult female.

**c. Below, Adult Male:** Buffy with fine black streaking. In flight, undersides appear dusky throughout. Throat and chest lightest. Wings dark. Tail with gray barring.

**d. Below, Adult Female:** Buffy with dark brown streaking. Appears very dark in flight. Tail with gray barring.

**Below, Immature** (not illustrated): Resembles adult female.

**e. Full Display:** Seldom seen in full display at Hawk Mountain except when it momentarily delays its direct flight to attack the owl decoy.

**f. Tuck:** Normally seen in this position. Typical falcon shape, but much more robust than kestrel and very dark.

**Could Be Confused With**

**American Kestrel:** Appears delicate by comparison; lacks merlin's robustness. Much lighter plumage. Distinct facial markings. Flight less determined, more fluttery and buoyant.

**Sharp-shinned Hawk:** Rounded wings. Lighter underparts overall. Flap-flap-flap—glide as opposed to strong, deep wingbeats.

**Lookout Tips**

Most merlins fly by quickly just south of the lookout. They appear and disappear in a flash. Merlins are uncommon along the ridges but common along the Atlantic Coast.

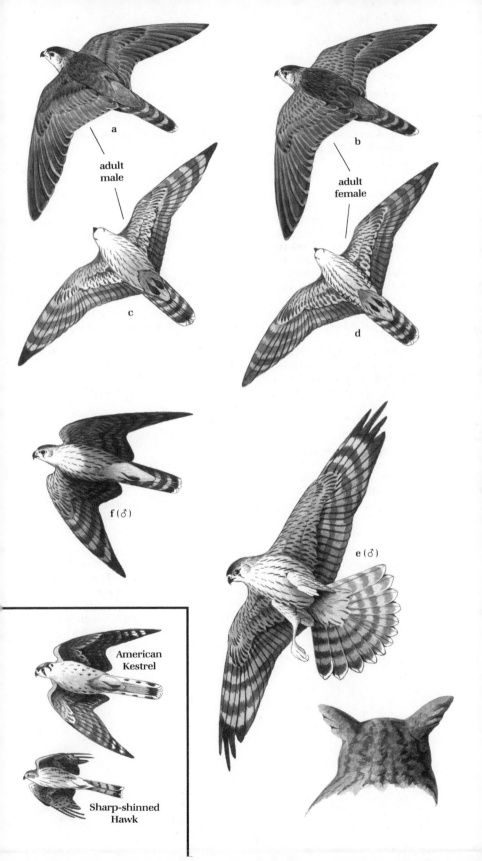

adult
male

a

adult
female

b

c

d

f (♂)

e (♂)

American
Kestrel

Sharp-shinned
Hawk

*Falco peregrinus*

**Overall Impression:** A large, stocky, long-winged falcon with a relatively short, broad tail that tapers from base to tip.

**In Flight:** Strong, determined, controlled flight. Powerful wingbeats. Wings seem to be snapped down after the upstroke. Occasionally seen soaring along the ridge.

## Position View

Barring and streaking on the underparts are highly variable.

**a. Above, Adult:** Blue-gray back and wings. Head with black crown. Distinctive moustache and black ear coverts. Tail with wide, black terminal band tipped in white; tip not often seen.

**b. Above, Immature:** Dark brown throughout except for paler brown crown. Less conspicuous moustache.

**c. Below, Adult:** Chin and throat buff. Lower breast and belly with narrow, black horizontal barring.

**d. Below, Immature:** Breast and belly buff with dark streaking, especially along the sides.

**e. Profile:** Long, swept-back wings and prominent moustache and black ear coverts are easily seen when viewed at or slightly above eye level.

**f. Head On:** Most striking in adult because of prominent facial markings. At close range facial patterns are distinct.

**g. Full Display:** When in full display, can be confused with broadwing, whose wings are shorter, or (at great heights) with kestrel, whose body is slim.

**h. Tuck (head on):** Same characteristics as for Profile.

**i. Tuck (below):** Wingtips extend along stocky body to end of tail.

## Could Be Confused With.

**Merlin:** Stockier body and shorter wings. Much darker overall. Typically, though by no means always, merlins pass to the right of the lookout, peregrines to the left.

**Goshawk (immature):** Much heftier body. Wings short compared with body length and tips rounded.

## Lookout Tips

Peregrine falcons are rare migrants along ridge systems; they occur more frequently—but still uncommonly—along the coast. Since Cornell University's Peregrine Fund began its captive-breeding and re-introduction program in the 1960s, more peregrines have been recorded along coastal migratory routes.

Peregrines fly past the lookout very quickly, offering little time for study. There is great excitement when a peregrine is sighted. Its identification and location will be shouted out, giving even the most inexperienced novice a chance to see it.

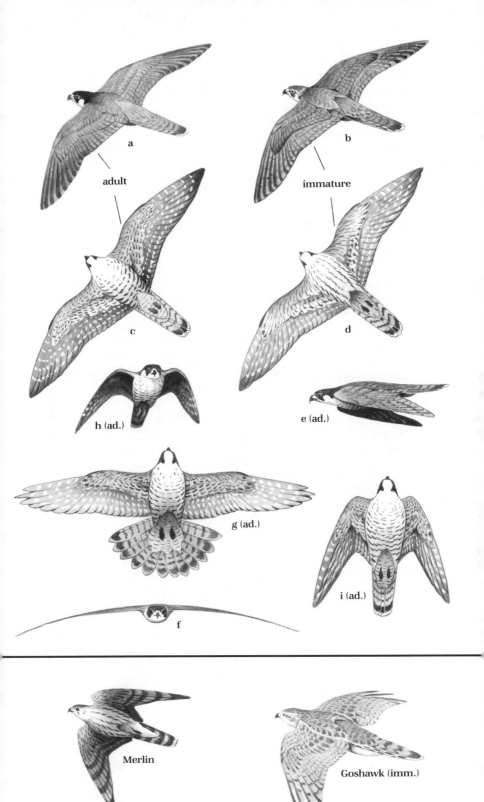

a

adult

b

immature

c

d

h (ad.)

e (ad.)

g (ad.)

i (ad.)

f

Merlin

Goshawk (imm.)

# Gyrfalcon

*Falco rusticolus*

**Overall Impression:** A very large falcon with broad-based wings and a moderately long tail that thickens near the bulky body. The gyrfalcon is Hawk Mountain's rarest migrant: few individuals have been recorded since 1934. Several have been recorded at other locations along the Kittatinny Ridge. The description and plate are included for persons with extensive field experience in raptor identification.

**In Flight:** The powerful flight seems slow, but the gyr can cover much ground with relatively few strokes. Wingtips appear splayed, not held tightly together as in other falcons.

## Position View

**a.** Above, White Morph: Overall plumage white with gray or black spotting or barring. Wings with gray barring and black tips.

**b.** Above, Gray or Dark Morph: A highly variable color morph. Slate or brown overall, or with darker crown and light forehead. Tail slate blue or brown with narrow dark bands or no obvious banding.

**c.** Below, White Morph: White underparts with dark tips on both primary and secondary wing feathers.

**d.** Below, Gray or Dark Morph: Chin to upper breast white or buff. Lower breast to belly and wings white with gray or brown spots and bars. Dark morph may be entirely dark.

**e.** Tuck: A larger version of peregrine falcon.

**f.** Full Display: Massiveness of this falcon apparent in full display configuration. Unfortunately, this position is rarely, if ever, seen from the North Lookout.

## Could Be Confused With

Goshawk (immature): On a glide, with wings pulled back, the goshawk wing extends barely beyond the body, whereas the gyrfalcon's wing extends nearly to the tip of the tail.

Peregrine Falcon: Sleeker, more streamlined. Wings narrow and pointed. More rapid flap.

white morph

gray or
dark morph

a

b

c

d

e

f

Goshawk
(imm.)

Peregrine
Falcon

# Northern Harrier

*Circus cyaneus*

**Overall Impression:** A medium-sized, slender-bodied raptor with long, narrow wings and tail and a prominent white rump.
**In Flight:** Buoyant flight. Rocks and tacks from side to side. Flaps in a slow rowing motion, then briefly glides with upheld wings. Wings held in a strong dihedral.

### Position View

**a. Above, Adult Male:** Gray to blue-gray throughout. Wingtips black. Rump feathers bright white.

**b. Above, Adult Female:** Crown dark brown, otherwise brown to tawny throughout. Rump feathers bright white.

**c. Below, Adult Male:** Neck to upper breast light gray, belly white. Underwing coverts white, otherwise wings gray throughout with broad black tips.

**d. Below, Adult Female:** Neck light gray to buff. Sides of face, breast heavily streaked with brown; lower belly buff. Dark brown wingtips.

**Below, Second-year Male** (not illustrated): Light buff underparts.

**Below, Second-year Female** (not illustrated): Upper breast with tawny to rufous spotting.

**Below, First-year Male and Female** (not illustrated): Chestnut to rufous underparts without spots or streaks.

Immatures of both sexes resemble adult females.

**e. Profile:** Wings held slightly forward in strong dihedral. Prominent white rump.

**f. Head On:** Slender-bodied with pronounced dihedral. Usually rocking or tacking.

**g. Tuck:** Rocks from side to side with gull-like flap using its long, narrow wings.

**h. Full Display:** A flight configuration seldom seen from the North Lookout, but shown when harrier soars over open farmland.

### Could Be Confused With

Harriers can be confused with any species that has prominent white feathers near the base of the tail—for example, the rough-legged hawk and golden eagle. Beware of the wrap-around undertail coverts of redtails and accipiters.

**Peregrine Falcon (immature):** Body stocky. Wings, when gliding or flapping, resemble the harrier's. Peregrine's flap is strong and determined; harrier's flap is leisurely, followed by a rocking glide.

**Golden Eagle (immature):** At great distances the basally white tail of an immature or subadult golden eagle can be mistaken for the harrier's white rump.

### Lookout Tips

Harriers seem to prefer the south side of the ridge, flapping and gliding above the trees toward the South Lookout. Others will cut low in front of the North Lookout, heading north over the Little Schuylkill River. The harrier migration spans the entire fall migration; the majority of adult males come last.

a

adult
male

b

adult
female

c

d

g
(ad. ♀ or imm.)

h
(ad. ♀ or imm.)

e
(ad. ♀ or imm.)

h (ad. ♂)

g
(ad. ♂)

f

Peregrine
Falcon (imm.)

Golden
Eagle (imm.)

# Osprey

*Pandion haliaetus*

**Overall Impression:** A large, black-and-white raptor with long, narrow, crooked wings held in a low-profile **M**. Head small, tail long.

**In Flight:** Most often seen in a glide with wings crooked and swept back. The faster the wind, the straighter the wing. On windless days, flies with deep, labored flaps. When it soars, wings are fully extended and tail spread.

## Position View

**a. Below, Adult Male:** White underparts. Lightly streaked upper breast. Bold black carpal (wrist) patches.

**b. Below, Adult Female:** White underparts with prominent brown necklace-like streaking on upper breast. (Owing to variations within populations, however, the degree of streaking is not a foolproof characteristic for sexing adults and is valid only about 50% of the time.) Bold black carpal patches. (Immatures may have buff on flanks through the first year.)

**c. Above, Male and Female (glide):** White forehead, otherwise brown throughout.

**d. Profile.**

**e. Head On:** Pronounced wing crook and white head make it one of the easiest raptors to identify.

**f. Full Display:** Wing crook reduced and tail spread while soaring in thermals.

## Could Be Confused With

At great distances ospreys can be confused with two other large birds, bald eagles and turkey vultures. Bald eagles exhibit a crook, and ospreys sometime exhibit a dihedral like that of turkey vultures, but vultures and eagles have dark undersides. Ospreys can also be confused with the gulls that sometimes soar in thermals above the ridges; however, gulls have a relatively larger head and proportionately longer wings.

## Lookout Tips

Ospreys migrate late in the day. During September great numbers will fly until dark. Seeing one after another migrating into a setting sun is splendid indeed.

On southerly or easterly winds, ospreys often cut away from the ridge and fly across the valley between the North Lookout and Hemlock Heights, flapping all the way. Occasionally, one flies past carrying a fish. When you become thoroughly proficient, you can also identify the fish!

a    adult male

b    adult female

c

d

e

f

Bald Eagle

Turkey Vulture

# Epilogue

Every raptor passing the North Lookout is a success story. The perils each faces, even before the first migration, are impressive. Many young raptors, for example, never become sufficiently skilled hunters to support themselves; they perish shortly after parental care ceases. What a feat it is to hatch in a Canadian forest, say, survive to leave the nesting ground, move across the United States, Mexico, Central America, and into the Andes, to survive a winter there, and then to negotiate the return trip the following spring. Some make it; many do not. Birds on migration cross boundaries both geographical and political. A raptor may enjoy a relatively safe breeding environment, then face serious stresses in its wintering range. Starvation and injury are always possible. Humans add to the dangers: habitat loss, pesticide application, shooting, and secondary poisoning are major threats to all birds of prey.

Hawk Mountain Sanctuary, the first refuge in the world to protect birds of prey, is a leader in raptor study and conservation. In the past few decades others have joined the fight, and there have been some notable successes. When the number of peregrine falcons dropped because of pesticide contamination of their food, biologists at Cornell University founded the Peregrine Fund to raise falcons in captivity and restock the wild. Peregrines now breed in the eastern United States, where they had been extirpated in 1970.

A different approach was taken with bald eagles—transfer instead of captive breeding. New York and Pennsylvania, among other states, obtained eaglets from Canada and Alaska and released them in areas where bald eagles historically nested. Wing-tagged immature eagles can now be seen flying by Hawk Mountain once or twice a year, visible proof of conservation in action.

A raptor that is not faring so well is the California condor, whose numbers declined drastically in this century. Biologists have netted the remaining birds—the last wild condor was captured in 1987—in the hope that the captive flock of twenty-seven will breed and their offspring can one day be released into the wild. This project has enjoyed success, as there are over forty condors in captivity now.

In the United States the combination of reintroduction programs and the ban on DDT and other persistent pesticides has been immensely successful in increasing the number of peregrine falcons, bald eagles, and ospreys throughout their historic ranges. And protection for birds of prey is spreading worldwide. Habitat protection in such places as the Snake River Birds of Prey Refuge in Idaho and the Philippines (for the Philippine eagle) are taking precedence. Migratory flyways are also the object of conservationists' efforts. But there is still much to be done. Destruction of habitat both in the breeding ranges and austral wintering grounds continues at an alarming rate.

Hawk Mountain Sanctuary's role in the conservation of birds of prey has been and continues to be education. It seemed to take forever to silence the guns, and the problems raptors and other wildlife face today are much more complex and difficult to deal with. But the organization and members who sustain the sanctuary have no choice but to respond to these problems. To do otherwise would be to ignore the sanctuary's roots and the mandate of its founders. The sanctuary continues to serve as a beacon for the conservation movement and as a refuge where people and birds meet a mountain.

# Life Cycles and
# Diets of the Raptors

Life cycles of the raptors that migrate past Hawk Mountain

| Species | Breed | Number of eggs | Incubation period (days) |
|---|---|---|---|
| Turkey vulture | Mar.–Apr. | 2 | 40 |
| Black vulture | Feb.–Mar. | 2 | 38 |
| Bald eagle | Sept.–Oct.* Mar.–Apr.† | 2–3 | 35 |
| Golden eagle | Mar.–May | 1–3 | 45 |
| Sharp-shinned hawk | Mar.–Apr. | 4–5 | 30 |
| Cooper's hawk | Mar.–Apr. | 4–5 | 36 |
| Northern goshawk | Mar.–Apr. | 2–4 | 32 |
| Red-tailed hawk | Feb.–Mar. | 2–3 | 34 |
| Red-shouldered hawk | Apr.–May | 3–4 | 33 |
| Broad-winged hawk | Late Apr.–May | 2–4 | 21–25 |
| Rough-legged hawk | May–June | 2–5 | 31 |
| Swainson's hawk | Apr.–May | 2–3 | 35 |
| American kestrel | Late Feb.–Apr. | 4–6 | 28 |
| Merlin | Apr.–May | 4–6 | 31 |
| Peregrine falcon | Mar.–Apr. | 3–4 | 35 |
| Gyrfalcon | Apr.–May | 3–4 | 36 |
| Northern harrier | Mar.–Apr. | 4–6 | 32 |
| Osprey | Apr. | 3 | 38 |

*Maryland and Virginia to Florida.
†Maine to Maryland.
‡In some years the number of migrants is higher than usual, indicating high productivity on the breeding grounds.
§Redtails seen during September—the broadwing season—are mostly local birds that have nested nearby in the summer and will stay in the area until October or November. Some individuals remain throughout the year.

| Fledge (days after hatching) | Reach independence (days after hatching) | Migrate south | Age at maturity (years) |
|---|---|---|---|
| 65 | 1 year | Nov. | 3 |
| 75 | 6–12 months | Local and transient | 3 |
| 77 | 112 | Aug.–Nov. | 4–5 |
| 65 | 120 | Oct.–Dec. | 4 |
| 35 | 7 weeks | late Aug.–Oct. | 2 |
| 34 | 53 | Sept.–early Nov. | 2 |
| 40 | 40 | Oct.—Dec. (cyclic)‡ | 2 |
| 45 | 100 | Sept.–Dec.§ | 2 |
| 45 | 70 | Sept.–Oct. | 2 |
| 40 | 40 | Aug.–Sept. | 2 |
| 41 | 60 | Oct.–Nov. (cyclic)‡ | 2 |
| 42 | 42 | Sept. (rare migrant) | 2 |
| 29 | 29 | Aug.–Oct. | 2 |
| 34 | 50–60 | Sept.–Oct. | 2 |
| 42 | 120 | Sept.–Oct. | 2 |
| 45 | 45 | Oct.–Nov. (very rare migrant) | 2 |
| 32 | 56 | Aug.–Nov. | 2 |
| 50 | 100 | Aug.–late Oct. | 3 |

# Diets of the raptors; prey are shown in order of preference and percentage taken

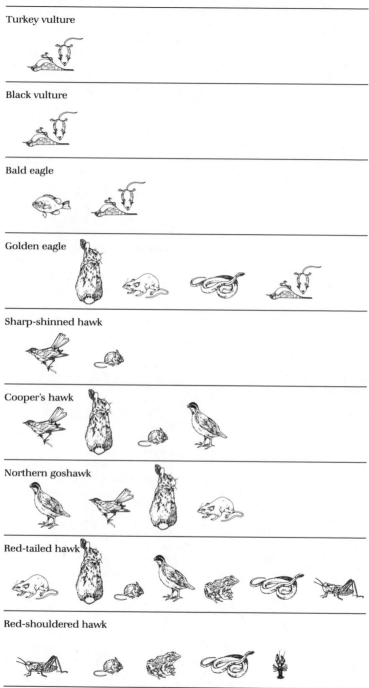

Turkey vulture

Black vulture

Bald eagle

Golden eagle

Sharp-shinned hawk

Cooper's hawk

Northern goshawk

Red-tailed hawk

Red-shouldered hawk

Adapted from an early National Audubon Society design in the Bird Leaflet Series (New York: National Audubon Society, 1945).

**Broad-winged hawk**

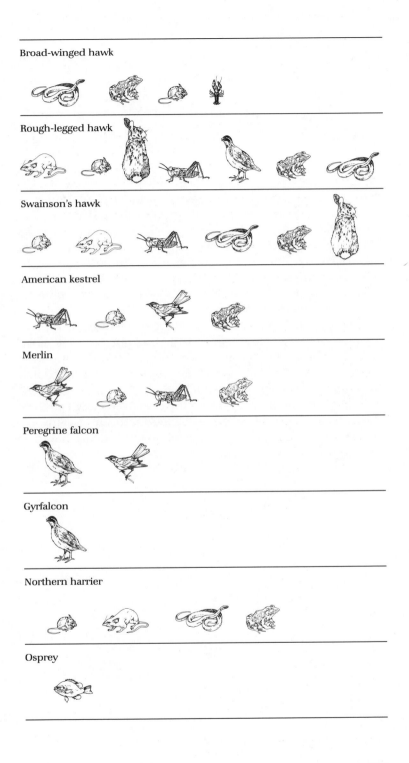

**Rough-legged hawk**

**Swainson's hawk**

**American kestrel**

**Merlin**

**Peregrine falcon**

**Gyrfalcon**

**Northern harrier**

**Osprey**

# Annual Migrant Raptor Counts at Hawk Mountain

Although the sizes of the raptor populations cannot be estimated from any single count at the North Lookout, trends in population size can be determined from the more than fifty years' worth of data collected since 1934. For example, counts of the bald eagle revealed that the average number of migrants decreased beginning in the late fifties and continuing through the sixties and seventies. DDT was found to be the cause, and after it was banned in the United States in 1972, eagle populations slowly began to recover.

The following table gives the number of migrant raptors counted at Hawk Mountain's North Lookout each fall since 1934, except for 1943–1945, when counts were discontinued because of World War II, and for 1967–1972, when counts from the South Lookout were included. The vultures are not counted because they remain in the area from early February through early November before drifting south, and Swainson's hawks and gyrfalcons are so rare at Hawk Mountain that their numbers are not given here.

| Year | Bald eagle | Golden eagle | Sharp-shinned | Cooper's | Goshawk | Red-tailed | Red-shouldered | Broad-winged | Rough-legged | Kestrel | Merlin | Pere-grine | Harrier | Osprey | Unid. | Totals |
|---|---|---|---|---|---|---|---|---|---|---|---|---|---|---|---|---|
| 1934 | 52 | 39 | 1,913 | 333 | 123 | 5,609 | 90 | 2,026 | 20 | 13 | 19 | 25 | 105 | 31 | 208 | 10,606 |
| 1935 | 67 | 66 | 4,237 | 553 | 293 | 4,024 | 181 | 5,459 | 9 | 123 | 20 | 14 | 153 | 169 | 23 | 15,391 |
| 1936 | 70 | 54 | 4,486 | 474 | 177 | 3,177 | 153 | 7,509 | 9 | 102 | 34 | 36 | 149 | 205 | 11 | 16,646 |
| 1937 | 38 | 73 | 4,817 | 492 | 49 | 4,978 | 163 | 4,500 | 4 | 141 | 10 | 41 | 160 | 201 | 8 | 15,675 |
| 1938 | 37 | 31 | 3,113 | 204 | 9 | 2,230 | 143 | 10,761 | 0 | 87 | 12 | 24 | 189 | 124 | 0 | 16,964 |
| 1939 | 64 | 83 | 8,529 | 590 | 26 | 6,496 | 314 | 5,736 | 8 | 184 | 43 | 38 | 273 | 174 | 0 | 22,558 |
| 1940 | 38 | 72 | 2,407 | 166 | 11 | 4,725 | 149 | 3,159 | 4 | 60 | 11 | 25 | 161 | 91 | 7 | 11,086 |
| 1941 | 50 | 55 | 3,909 | 416 | 21 | 4,700 | 198 | 5,170 | 2 | 196 | 35 | 44 | 254 | 201 | 38 | 15,289 |
| 1942* | 71 | 35 | 3,203 | 292 | 9 | 2,378 | 120 | 4,362 | 0 | 113 | 17 | 36 | 107 | 213 | 38 | 10,802 |
| 1946 | 42 | 69 | 2,409 | 221 | 32 | 2,358 | 248 | 3,280 | 0 | 98 | 20 | 26 | 171 | 191 | 62 | 9,227 |
| 1947 | 92 | 34 | 1,745 | 122 | 5 | 1,677 | 245 | 7,791 | 0 | 121 | 10 | 19 | 176 | 297 | 52 | 12,386 |
| 1948 | 88 | 40 | 1,651 | 203 | 14 | 2,499 | 268 | 15,454 | 10 | 142 | 19 | 33 | 186 | 170 | 96 | 20,873 |
| 1949 | 98 | 47 | 2,908 | 174 | 7 | 2,736 | 283 | 9,636 | 16 | 334 | 20 | 33 | 212 | 212 | 55 | 16,771 |
| 1950 | 142 | 68 | 3,719 | 263 | 6 | 2,669 | 346 | 6,638 | 2 | 253 | 45 | 35 | 223 | 323 | 120 | 14,852 |
| 1951 | 100 | 54 | 3,039 | 238 | 21 | 2,292 | 378 | 11,132 | 0 | 257 | 15 | 26 | 222 | 254 | 67 | 18,095 |
| 1952 | 114 | 80 | 3,559 | 308 | 7 | 2,555 | 347 | 12,629 | 9 | 210 | 45 | 32 | 309 | 343 | 73 | 20,620 |
| 1953 | 60 | 31 | 3,018 | 165 | 4 | 2,193 | 199 | 7,270 | 2 | 223 | 11 | 15 | 238 | 341 | 140 | 13,910 |
| 1954 | 77 | 40 | 3,220 | 194 | 96 | 2,072 | 311 | 5,911 | 3 | 176 | 28 | 29 | 151 | 336 | 93 | 12,737 |
| 1955 | 89 | 57 | 4,381 | 282 | 37 | 3,802 | 428 | 9,957 | 0 | 276 | 23 | 35 | 230 | 359 | 173 | 20,129 |
| 1956 | 54 | 48 | 2,079 | 122 | 7 | 1,537 | 318 | 8,748 | 10 | 192 | 10 | 19 | 138 | 288 | 45 | 13,615 |
| 1957 | 39 | 46 | 2,674 | 203 | 81 | 2,744 | 216 | 8,949 | 8 | 175 | 22 | 15 | 187 | 319 | 98 | 15,776 |
| 1958 | 46 | 41 | 1,765 | 176 | 20 | 2,956 | 470 | 8,880 | 1 | 219 | 19 | 25 | 203 | 321 | 108 | 15,250 |
| 1959 | 41 | 31 | 2,819 | 170 | 25 | 1,911 | 344 | 5,282 | 12 | 281 | 17 | 33 | 257 | 288 | 82 | 11,593 |
| 1960 | 37 | 38 | 2,395 | 159 | 15 | 2,317 | 377 | 12,585 | 30 | 236 | 33 | 26 | 290 | 303 | 52 | 18,893 |
| 1961 | 51 | 52 | 1,753 | 108 | 89 | 2,606 | 333 | 8,403 | 36 | 470 | 13 | 23 | 283 | 352 | 117 | 14,689 |
| 1962 | 48 | 40 | 2,283 | 77 | 33 | 2,748 | 268 | 8,276 | 7 | 446 | 20 | 30 | 186 | 290 | 110 | 14,862 |
| 1963 | 30 | 28 | 1,532 | 73 | 28 | 3,474 | 210 | 9,474 | 11 | 265 | 27 | 21 | 178 | 190 | 101 | 15,642 |
| 1964 | 28 | 28 | 1,314 | 62 | 19 | 2,799 | 223 | 10,218 | 16 | 237 | 11 | 21 | 191 | 328 | 28 | 15,523 |
| 1965 | 43 | 34 | 3,498 | 103 | 102 | 3,305 | 303 | 9,318 | 4 | 408 | 23 | 14 | 190 | 444 | 113 | 17,902 |
| 1966 | 32 | 16 | 2,947 | 84 | 30 | 2,578 | 314 | 10,268 | 4 | 579 | 26 | 22 | 178 | 405 | 311 | 17,794 |

| Year | Bald eagle | Golden eagle | Sharp-shinned | Cooper's | Goshawk | Red-tailed | Red-shouldered | Broad-winged | Rough-legged | Kestrel | Merlin | Peregrine | Harrier | Osprey | Unid. | Totals |
|---|---|---|---|---|---|---|---|---|---|---|---|---|---|---|---|---|
| 1967† | 38 | 36 | 3,243 | 101 | 32 | 2,680 | 374 | 12,052 | 7 | 666 | 20 | 22 | 244 | 457 | 221 | 20,193 |
| 1968† | 55 | 39 | 3,677 | 220 | 233 | 4,647 | **512** | 18,507 | 6 | 736 | 21 | 21 | 480 | 403 | 206 | 29,763 |
| 1969† | 41 | 28 | 3,708 | 145 | 146 | 4,338 | 296 | 12,901 | 15 | 610 | 32 | 26 | 321 | 530 | 282 | 23,419 |
| 1970† | 28 | 25 | 3,405 | 144 | 107 | 3,632 | 350 | 14,372 | 18 | 521 | 23 | 27 | **495** | 600 | 253 | 24,000 |
| 1971† | 32 | 35 | 4,239 | 123 | 61 | 3,673 | 400 | 11,573 | 23 | 564 | 22 | 22 | 462 | 613 | 335 | 22,177 |
| 1972† | 23 | 43 | 3,867 | 142 | **428** | 4,290 | 231 | 16,621 | 7 | 475 | 11 | 10 | 294 | 486 | 309 | 27,237 |
| 1973 | 17 | 46 | 3,347 | 81 | 307 | 3,098 | 116 | 6,404 | 8 | 479 | 13 | 9 | 177 | 346 | 166 | 14,614 |
| 1974 | 13 | 27 | 4,477 | 150 | 61 | 3,658 | 182 | 9,146 | 17 | 434 | 10 | 7 | 163 | 183 | 69 | 18,597 |
| 1975 | 19 | 27 | 5,354 | 126 | 136 | 2,880 | 205 | 10,390 | 9 | 487 | 19 | 6 | 267 | 196 | 160 | 20,281 |
| 1976 | 18 | 40 | 5,376 | 109 | 62 | 3,694 | 167 | 8,461 | 13 | 413 | 20 | 8 | 248 | 314 | 182 | 19,125 |
| 1977 | 18 | 28 | **10,473** | 231 | 82 | 3,385 | 264 | 13,009 | 15 | 705 | 27 | 11 | 282 | 340 | 231 | 29,101 |
| 1978 | 27 | 29 | 6,827 | 183 | 57 | 2,848 | 163 | **29,523** | 7 | 370 | 16 | 9 | 183 | 378 | 107 | **40,727** |
| 1979 | 14 | 35 | 10,305 | 336 | 68 | 4,173 | 234 | 11,173 | 14 | 540 | 52 | 14 | 236 | 442 | 141 | 27,777 |
| 1980 | 22 | 65 | 8,313 | 374 | 85 | 5,720 | 349 | 10,141 | 23 | 529 | 29 | 9 | 466 | 360 | 115 | 26,600 |
| 1981 | 28 | 53 | 9,463 | 756 | 138 | 3,939 | 250 | 8,660 | 18 | 709 | 47 | 20 | 280 | 537 | 188 | 25,086 |
| 1982 | 36 | 54 | 4,576 | 303 | 141 | 5,027 | 320 | 7,452 | 17 | 414 | 19 | 6 | 295 | 435 | 155 | 19,250 |
| 1983 | 23 | 57 | 6,517 | 352 | 129 | 3,955 | 451 | 6,922 | 14 | 461 | 21 | 7 | 318 | 454 | 243 | 19,924 |
| 1984 | 40 | 36 | 3,799 | 171 | 60 | 3,158 | 210 | 13,655 | 5 | 347 | 21 | 8 | 318 | 589 | 184 | 22,601 |
| 1985 | 37 | 58 | 5,764 | 288 | 52 | 2,875 | 205 | 3,415 | 12 | 383 | 37 | 12 | 367 | 399 | 255 | 14,159 |
| 1986 | 56 | 44 | 9,236 | 569 | 106 | 3,308 | 175 | 13,932 | 11 | 455 | 78 | 24 | 304 | 798 | 200 | 29,296 |
| 1987 | 65 | **98** | 6,773 | 588 | 57 | 4,215 | 349 | 8,409 | 24 | 577 | 50 | 31 | 355 | 660 | 117 | 22,368 |
| 1988 | 57 | 67 | 6,718 | 457 | 50 | 4,705 | 365 | 5,933 | 14 | 634 | 49 | 15 | 304 | 611 | 130 | 20,109 |
| 1989 | 62 | 45 | 9,833 | **787** | 27 | 3,712 | 260 | 7,504 | 12 | **839** | **157** | **51** | 402 | 758 | 137 | 24,586 |
| 1990 | 73 | 80 | 8,130 | 643 | 89 | 3,786 | 329 | 4,742 | 21 | 728 | 144 | 49 | 320 | **873** | 239 | 20,246 |

*Note:* Numbers shown in boldface type are record numbers at Hawk Mountain. Unid. = unidentified.

*No counts taken during 1943–1945.

†Caution should be used in interpretations of the data for 1967–1972. In 1967 the South Lookout was opened, and the counts for 1967–1972 include the birds sighted at both the North and South lookouts. Since 1973 the counts have been conducted only at the North Lookout. Hawk Mountain researchers have excluded South Lookout numbers from all trend analyses.

# Checklist of Plants and Animals at Hawk Mountain

## PLANTS

### Ferns and Fern Allies

Wolf's Claw Clubmoss *Lycopodium clavatum*
Running Pine *Lycopodium complanatum*
Bog Clubmoss *Lycopodium inundatum*
Shining Clubmoss *Lycopodium lucidulum*
Ground Pine *Lycopodium obscurum*
Field Horsetail *Equisetum arvense*
Cut-leaved Grape Fern *Botrychium dissectum*
Daisy-leaf Grape Fern *Botrychium matricariifolium*
Rattlesnake Fern *Botrychium virginianum*
Cinnamon Fern *Osmunda cinnamomea*
Interrupted Fern *Osmunda claytoniana*
Royal Fern *Osmunda regalis*
Maidenhair Fern *Adiantum pedatum*
Ebony Spleenwort *Asplenium platyneuron*
Maidenhair Spleenwort *Asplenium trichomanes*
Lady Fern *Athyrium filix-femina*
Silvery Spleenwort *Athyrium thelypteroides*
Walking Fern *Camptosorus rhizophyllus*
Fragile Fern *Cystopteris fragilis*
Hay-scented Fern *Dennstaedtia punctilobula*
Spinulose Woodfern *Dryopteris spinulosa*
Marginal Shield Fern *Dryopteris marginalis*
American Shield Fern *Dryopteris intermedia*
Ostrich Fern *Matteuccia struthiopteris*
Sensitive Fern *Onoclea sensibilis*
Purple-stemmed Cliffbrake *Pellaea atropurpurea*
Common Polypody *Polypodium vulgare*
Christmas Fern *Polystrichum acrostichoides*
Bracken Fern *Pteridium aquilinum*
New York Fern *Thelypteris noveboracensis*
Broad Beech Fern *Thelypteris hexagonoptera*
Blunt-lobed Woodsia *Woodsia obtusa*
Virginia Chain Fern *Woodwardia virginica*

### Trees

Pitch Pine *Pinus rigida*
White Pine *Pinus strobus*
Eastern Hemlock *Tsuga canadensis*
Trembling Aspen *Populus tremuloides*
Large-toothed Aspen *Populus grandidentata*
Shag-bark Hickory *Carya ovata*
Mockernut Hickory *Carya tomentosa*
Bitternut Hickory *Carya cordiformis*
Pignut Hickory *Carya glabra*
Black Walnut *Juglans nigra*
Smooth Alder *Alnus rugosa*
Sweet Birch *Betula lenta*

Yellow Birch *Betula alleghaniensis*
River Birch *Betula nigra*
Gray Birch *Betula populifolia*
American Hazelnut *Corylus americana*
American Chestnut *Castanea dentata*
Beech *Fagus grandifolia*
White Oak *Quercus alba*
Scarlet Oak *Quercus coccinea*
Scrub Oak *Quercus ilicifolia*
Chestnut Oak *Quercus prinus*
Red Oak *Quercus rubra*
Tulip Tree *Liriodendron tulipifera*
Sassafras *Sassafras albidum*
Witch Hazel *Hamamelis virginiana*
American Mountain Ash *Sorbus americana*
Shadbush *Amelanchier intermedia arborea*
Fire Cherry *Prunus pensylvanica*
Black Cherry *Prunus serotina*
Choke Cherry *Prunus virginiana*
Staghorn Sumac *Rhus typhina*
Red Maple *Acer rubrum*
Striped Maple *Acer pensylvanicum*
Black Gum *Nyssa sylvatica*
Flowering Dogwood *Cornus florida*
Red-osier Dogwood *Cornus stolonifera*
Persimmon *Diospyros virginiana*
White Ash *Fraxinus americana*
Northern Catalpa *Catalpa speciosa*

### Shrubs

Sweet Fern *Comptonia peregrina*
Multiflora Rose *Rosa multiflora*
Black Raspberry *Rubus occidentalis*
Spice Bush *Lindera benzoin*
Poison Ivy *Rhus radicans*
Mountain Holly
 *Ilex montana*
 *Ilex opaca*
 *Ilex verticillata*
 *Nemopanthus mucronata*
Bittersweet *Celastrus scandens*
Virginia Creeper *Parthenocissus quinquefolia*
Fox Grape *Vitis labrusca*
Frost Grape *Vitis vulpina*
Autumn Olive *Elaeagnus umbellata*
Huckleberry *Gaylussacia baccata*
Mountain Laurel *Kalmia latifolia*
Sheep Laurel *Kalmia angustifolia*
Rhododendron *Rhododendron maximum*
High-bush Huckleberry *Vaccinium corymbosum*
Low-bush Blueberry *Vaccinium angustifolium*
Partridge Berry *Mitchella repens*

Tartarian Honeysuckle *Lonicera tatarica*
Common Elderberry *Sambucus canadensis*

## Flowers of the Forest and Forest Edge

Jack-in-the-Pulpit *Arisaema triphyllum*
Lily-of-the-Valley *Convallaria majalis*
Day Lily *Hemerocallis fulva* A
Trout Lily *Erythronium americanum*
Wild Lily-of-the-Valley *Maianthemum canadense*
Indian Cucumber *Medeola virginiana*
False Solomon's Seal *Smilacina racemosa*
Great Solomon's Seal *Polygonatum canaliculatum*
Greenbrier *Smilax rotundifolia*
Carrion-flower *Smilax herbacea*
Painted Trillium *Trillium undulatum*
Pink Lady's Slipper *Cypripedium acaule*
Yellow-fringed Orchis *Habenaria ciliaris*
Ragged-fringed Orchis *Habenaria lacera*
Showy Orchis *Orchis spectabilis*
Downy Rattlesnake Plantain *Goodyera pubescens*
Whorled Pogonia *Isotria verticillata*
Lamb's Quarters *Chenopodium album*
Pokeweed *Phytolacca americana*
Spring Beauty *Claytonia virginica*
Deptford Pink *Dianthus armeria* A
Starry Campion *Silene stellata*
Bladder Campion *Silene cacubalus*
Fire Pink *Silene virginica*
Bugbane *Cimicifuga racemosa*
Wild Columbine *Aquilegia canadensis*
Hepatica *Hepatica americana*
May Apple *Podophyllum peltatum*
Bloodroot *Sanguinaria canadensis*
Celandine *Chelidonium majus* A
Common Wintercress *Barbarea vulgaris* A
Round-leaved Sundew *Drosera rotundifolia*
Common Cinquefoil *Potentilla simplex*
Crown Vetch *Coronilla varia* A
Rabbit's-foot Clover *Trifolium arvense* A
Red Clover *Trifolium pratense* A
White Clover *Trifolium repens* A
Common Wood Sorrel *Oxalis montana*
Yellow Wood Sorrel *Oxalis europaea*
Erect Wood Sorrel *Oxalis stricta*
Fringed Polygala *Polygala paucifolia*
Spotted Touch-Me-Not *Impatiens capensis*
Pale Touch-Me-Not *Impatiens pallida*
Northern Blue Violet *Viola septentrionalis*
Sweet White Violet *Viola blanda*
Downy Yellow Violet *Viola pubescens*
Bristly Sarsaparilla *Aralia hispida*
Dwarf Ginseng *Panax trifolium*
Round-leaved Pyrola *Pyrola rotundifolia*
Pipsissewa *Chimaphila umbellata*
Spotted Wintergreen *Chimaphila maculata*
Trailing Arbutus *Epigaea repens*
Indian-Pipe *Monotropa uniflora*
Pine-Sap *Monotropa hypopithys*
Pimpernel *Anagallis arvensis* A
Whorled Loosetrife *Lysimachia quadrifolia*
Starflower *Trientalis borealis*
Butterfly-weed *Asclepias tuberosa*
Common Milkweed *Asclepias syriaca*
Swamp Milkweed *Asclepias incarnata*
Viper's Bugloss *Echium vulgare* A
Gill-over-the-Ground *Glechoma hederacea* A

Basil Balm *Monarda clinopodia*
Wild Bergamot *Monarda fistulosa*
Selfheal *Prunella vulgaris* A
Common Mullein *Verbascum thapsus* A
Common Speedwell *Veronica officinalis* A
Squawroot *Conopholis americana*
Venus' Looking-glass *Specularia perfoliata*
Cardinal Flower *Lobelia cardinalis*
Pearly Everlasting *Anaphalis margaritacea*
Common Ragweed *Ambrosia artemisiifolia*
Common Burdock *Arctium minus* A
Spotted Knapweed *Centaurea maculosa* A
Wild Lettuce *Lactuca canadensis*
Wavy-leaved Aster *Aster undulatus*
Large-leaved Aster *Aster macrophyllus*
Sweet Joe-Pye Weed *Eupatorium purpureum*
Trumpetweed *Eupatorium fistulosum*
White Snakeroot *Eupatorium rugosum*
Daisy Fleabane *Erigeron annuus*
Woodland Sunflower *Helianthus strumosus*
Bull Thistle *Cirsium vulgare* A
Canada Thistle *Cirsium arvense* A
Common Chicory *Cichorium intybus* A
Orange Hawkweed *Hieracium aurantiacum* A
Mouse-ear Hawkweed *Hieracium pilosella* A
Rattlesnake Weed *Hieracium venosum*
Two-flowered Cynthia *Krigia biflora*
Downy Goldenrod *Solidago puberula*

A = Alien.

Nomenclature after Edgar T. Wherry,
John M. Fogg, Jr., and Herbert A. Wahl, *Atlas of the Flora of Pennsylvania* (Philadelphia: The Morris Arboretum of the University of Pennsylvania, 1979).

## REPTILES AND AMPHIBIANS

Snapping Turtle *Chelydra serpentina*
Spotted Turtle *Clemmys guttata*
Wood Turtle *Clemmys insculpta*
Eastern Box Turtle *Terrapene carolina carolina*
Midland Painted Turtle *Chrysemys picta marginata*
Northern Water Snake *Natrix sipedon*
Northern Brown Snake *Storeria dekayi*
Eastern Garter Snake *Thamnophis sirtalis*
Eastern Hognose Snake *Heterodon platyrhinos*
Northern Ringneck Snake *Diadophis punctatus*
Northern Black Racer *Coluber constrictor*
Smooth Green Snake *Opheodrys vernalis*
Black Rat Snake *Elaphe obsoleta*
Eastern Milk Snake *Lampropeltis triangulum*
Northern Copperhead *Agkistrodon contortrix*
Timber Rattlesnake *Crotalus horridus*
Five-lined Skink *Eumeces fasciatus*
Spotted Salamander *Ambystoma maculatum*
Red-spotted Newt *Diemictylus viridescens*
Northern Dusky Salamander *Desmognathus fuscus*
Red-backed Salamander *Plethodon cinereus cinereus*\*
Slimy Salamander *Plethodon glutinosus*
Spring Salamander *Gyrinophilus porphyriticus*
Northern Red Salamander *Pseudotriton ruber*

Northern Two-lined Salamander *Eurycea bislineata*
American Toad *Bufo americanus*
Northern Cricket Frog *Acris crepitans*
Spring Peeper *Hyla crucifer*
Gray Treefrog *Hyla versicolor*
Bullfrog *Rana catesbeiana*
Green Frog *Rana clamitans melanota*
Pickerel Frog *Rana palustris*
Wood Frog *Rana sylvatica*

*Also occurs in a dark color phase known as the Lead-backed Salamander.

Nomenclature after Roger Conant, *A Field Guide to Reptiles and Amphibians of Eastern and Central North America,* 2nd ed. (Boston: Houghton Mifflin, 1975).

## MAMMALS

Virginia Opossum *Didelphis virginiana*
Masked Shrew *Sorex cinereus*
Smoky Shrew *Sorex fumeus*
Least Shrew *Cryptotis parva*
Northern Short-tailed Shrew *Blarina brevicauda*
Little Brown Myotis *Myotis lucifugus*
Big Brown Bat *Eptesicus fuscus*
Red Bat *Lasiurus borealis**
Black Bear *Ursus americanus*
Raccoon *Procyon lotor*

Long-tailed Weasel *Mustela frenata*
Mink *Mustela vison*
Striped Skunk *Mephitis mephitis*
Coyote *Canis latrans*
Gray Fox *Urocyon cinereoargenteus*
Red Fox *Vulpes vulpes fulva*
Bobcat *Lynx rufus*
Woodchuck *Marmota monax*
Eastern Chipmunk *Tamias striatus*
Eastern Gray Squirrel *Sciurus carolinensis*
Eastern Fox Squirrel *Sciurus niger*†
Red Squirrel *Tamiasciurus hudsonicus*
Southern Flying Squirrel *Glaucomys volans*
Beaver *Castor canadensis*
White-footed Mouse *Peromyscus leucopus*
Boreal Redback Vole *Clethrionomys gapperi gapperi*
Meadow Vole *Microtus pennsylvanicus*
Woodland Jumping Mouse *Napaeozapus insignis*
Porcupine *Erethizon dorsatum*
Eastern Cottontail *Sylvilagus floridanus*
Virginia Whitetail Deer *Odocoileus virginianus*

*Seen migrating during the fall.
†Recorded once on the sanctuary.
Nomenclature after William H. Burt, *A Field Guide to the Mammals,* 3rd ed. (Boston: Houghton Mifflin, 1976).

## BIRDS

This list is based on observations made within the sanctuary and the Pine Swamp and Little Schuylkill River environs since 1934.

| | Sp | S | F | W |
|---|---|---|---|---|
| Red-throated Loon *Gavia stellata* | um | | cm | |
| Common Loon *Gavia immer* | | | rm | |
| Red-necked Grebe *Podiceps grisegena* | a | | | |
| Double-crested Cormorant *Phalacrocorax auritus* | rm | | rm | |
| American Bittern *Botaurus lentiginosus* | r | r | r | |
| Great Blue Heron *Ardea herodias* | r | u | um | r |
| Great Egret *Casmerodius albus* | | r | | |
| Snowy Egret *Egretta thula* | | | a | |
| Tricolored Heron *Egretta tricolor* | a | | | |
| Green-backed Heron *Butorides striatus* | u* | u | u | |
| Black-crowned Night-Heron *Nycticorax nycticorax* | o | | rm | |
| Yellow-crowned Night-Heron *Nycticorax violacea* | | a | | |
| Glossy Ibis *Plegadis falcinellus* | rm | | rm | |
| White Ibis *Eudocimus albus* | | | a | |
| Tundra Swan *Cygnus columbianus* | | | om | |
| Mute Swan *Cygnus olor* | | t | | |
| Snow Goose *Chen caerulescens* | | | om | |
| "Blue" Goose *Chen caerulescens* | | | a | |
| Canada Goose *Branta canadensis* | c* | c | cm | u |
| Brant *Branta bernicla* | om | | um | |
| Wood Duck *Aix sponsa* | o* | t | u | |
| Mallard *Anas platyrhynchos* | c* | c | c | |
| American Black Duck *Anas rubripes* | r* | t | om | |
| Northern Pintail *Anas acuta* | r | t | om | |
| Green-winged Teal *Anas crecca* | | | rm | |
| Blue-winged Teal *Anas discors* | | | rm | |
| American Wigeon *Anas americana* | | | rm | |
| Redhead *Aythya americana* | | | a | |
| Canvasback *Aythya valisineria* | | | rm | |
| Lesser Scaup *Aythya affinis* | | | a | |
| Bufflehead *Bucephala albeola* | am | | am | |
| Oldsquaw *Clangula hyemalis* | | | rm | |
| White-winged Scoter *Melanitta fusca* | | | rm | |
| Black Scoter *Melanitta nigra* | | | rm | |
| Red-breasted Merganser *Mergus serrator* | | | a | |
| Common Merganser *Mergus merganser* | om | | om | |
| Black Vulture *Coragyps atratus* | o* | u | u | |
| Turkey Vulture *Cathartes aura* | c* | c | c | u |
| Osprey *Pandion haliaetus* | t | | cm | |
| Bald Eagle *Haliaeetus leucocephalus* | um | t | um | t |
| Northern Harrier *Circus cyaneus* | rm | r | cm | o |
| Sharp-shinned Hawk *Accipiter striatus* | cm* | c | cm | u |
| Cooper's Hawk *Accipiter cooperii* | om* | r | cm | u |
| Northern Goshawk *Accipiter gentilis* | o* | o | cm | o |
| Red-shouldered Hawk *Buteo lineatus* | om* | r | cm | t |
| Broad-winged Hawk *Buteo platypterus* | cm* | c | cm | |
| Swainson's Hawk *Buteo swainsoni* | | | rm | |
| Red-tailed Hawk *Buteo jamaicensis* | c* | c | cm | c |
| Rough-legged Hawk *Buteo lagopus* | rm | | rm | t |
| Golden Eagle *Aquila chrysaetos* | rm | | om | t |
| American Kestrel (P) *Falco sparverius* | cm* | c | cm | c |
| Merlin *Falco columbarius* | rm | | om | t |
| Peregrine Falcon *Falco peregrinus* | rm | | om | t |
| Gyrfalcon *Falco rusticolus* | | | rm | |
| Ring-necked Pheasant (P) *Phasianus colchicus* | o* | o | o | o |
| Ruffed Grouse (P) *Bonasa umbellus* | o* | o | o | o |
| Turkey (P) *Meleagris gallopavo* | o* | o | o | o |
| Northern Bobwhite *Colinus virginianus* | r | r | r | |
| Virginia Rail *Rallus limicola* | a | | | |
| Sora *Porzana carolina* | | | a | |
| American Coot *Fulica americana* | | | rm | |
| Sandhill Crane *Grus canadensis* | rm | | rm | |

| | Sp | S | F | W |
|---|---|---|---|---|
| Black-bellied Plover *Pluvialis squatarola* | | | rm | |
| Lesser Golden-Plover *Pluvialis dominica* | | | rm | |
| Killdeer *Charadrius vociferus* | u* | o | rm | |
| American Avocet *Recurvirostra americana* | | | a | |
| Greater Yellowlegs *Tringa melanoleuca* | | | om | |
| Lesser Yellowlegs *Tringa flavipes* | | | om | |
| Solitary Sandpiper *Tringa solitaria* | a | | rm | |
| Willet *Catoptrophorus semipalmatus* | | | a | |
| Upland Sandpiper *Bartramia longicauda* | r | r | | |
| Spotted Sandpiper *Actitis macularia* | rm | | rm | |
| Ruddy Turnstone *Arenaria interpres* | | | a | |
| Semipalmated Sandpiper *Calidris pusillus* | | | rm | |
| Least Sandpiper *Calidris minutilla* | | | a | |
| Pectoral Sandpiper *Calidris melanotos* | | | rm | |
| Dunlin *Calidris alpina* | | | rm | |
| Long-billed Dowitcher *Limnodromus scolopaceus* | | | a | |
| Common Snipe *Gallinago gallinago* | | r | rm | r |
| American Woodcock *Scolopax minor* | u* | r | r | |
| Bonaparte's Gull *Larus philadelphia* | a | | rm | |
| Ring-billed Gull *Larus delawarensis* | | | om | |
| Herring Gull *Larus argentatus* | | | om | |
| Great Black-backed Gull *Larus marinus* | | | a | |
| Sabine's Gull *Xema sabini* | | | a | |
| Common Tern *Sterna hirundo* | | | a | |
| Rock Dove *Columba livia* | t | t | t | t |
| Mourning Dove (P) *Zenaida macroura* | c* | c | c | c |
| Black-billed Cuckoo *Coccyzus erythropthalmus* | u* | u | | |
| Yellow-billed Cuckoo *Coccyzus americanus* | u* | u | | |
| Common Barn Owl *Tyto alba* | r | r | r | r |
| Eastern Screech Owl (P) *Otus asio* | c* | c | c | c |
| Great Horned Owl (P) *Bubo virginianus* | c* | c | c | c |
| Barred Owl (P) *Strix varia* | u* | u | u | r |
| Long-eared Owl *Asio otus* | | r | r | r |
| Short-eared Owl *Asio flammeus* | r | | r | r |
| Northern Saw-whet Owl (P) *Aegolius acadicus* | r* | o | o | o |
| Common Nighthawk *Chordeiles minor* | um | t | um | |
| Whip-poor-will† *Caprimulgus vociferus* | rm | o | rm | |
| Chimney Swift *Chaetura pelagica* | o* | o | cm | |
| Ruby-throated Hummingbird *Archilochus colubris* | c* | c | cm | |
| Belted Kingfisher (P) *Ceryle alcyon* | c* | c | c | c |
| Red-headed Woodpecker *Melanerpes erythrocephalus* | um | u | um | u |
| Red-bellied Woodpecker (P) *Melanerpes carolinus* | u* | u | u | u |
| Yellow-bellied Sapsucker *Sphyrapicus varius* | om | | om | r |
| Downy Woodpecker (P) *Picoides pubescens* | c* | c | c | c |
| Hairy Woodpecker (P) *Picoides villosus* | o* | o | o | o |
| Black-backed Woodpecker *Picoides arcticus* | | | a | |
| Northern Flicker *Colaptes auratus* | c* | c | cm | |
| Pileated Woodpecker (P) *Dryocopus pileatus* | u* | u | u | u |
| Olive-sided Flycatcher *Contopus borealis* | om | t | om | |
| Eastern Wood-Pewee (P) *Contopus virens* | cm* | c | om | |
| Yellow-bellied Flycatcher *Empidonax flaviventris* | om | t | om | |
| Acadian Flycatcher *Empidonax virescens* | o* | r | rm | |
| Alder Flycatcher *Empidonax alnorum* | rm | t | rm | |
| Least Flycatcher *Empidonax minimus* | om* | o | om | |
| Eastern Phoebe *Sayornis phoebe* | c* | c | um | |
| Great Crested Flycatcher *Myiarchus crinitus* | c* | c | u | |
| Eastern Kingbird *Tyrannus tyrannus* | u* | o | r | |
| Horned Lark *Eremophila alpestris* | | | om | t |
| Purple Martin *Progne subis* | r* | t | um | |
| Tree Swallow *Tachycineta bicolor* | cm* | u | cm | |
| No. Rough-winged Swallow *Stelgidopteryx serripennis* | rm | u | om | |
| Bank Swallow *Riparia riparia* | om* | t | om | |
| Cliff Swallow *Hirundo pyrrhonota* | um* | t | om | |
| Barn Swallow *Hirundo rustica* | cm* | c | um | |
| Blue Jay (P) *Cyanocitta cristata* | cm* | c | cm | c |
| American Crow *Corvus brachyrhynchos* | cm* | c | cm | c |
| Fish Crow *Corvus ossifragus* | o | | o | |
| Common Raven *Corvus corax* | t | t | um | |

109

|  | Sp | S | F | W |
|---|---|---|---|---|
| Black-capped Chickadee (P) *Parus atricapillus* | c* | c | c | c |
| Carolina Chickadee *Parus carolinensis* |  |  |  | a |
| Boreal Chickadee *Parus hudsonicus* | a |  | a |  |
| Tufted Titmouse (P) *Parus bicolor* | c* | c | c | c |
| Red-breasted Nuthatch *Sitta canadensis* | o | t | um | u |
| White-breasted Nuthatch (P) *Sitta carolinensis* | c* | c | c | c |
| Brown Creeper (P) *Certhia americana* | u* | u | u | u |
| Carolina Wren *Thryothorus ludovicianus* | o* | o | o | o |
| Bewick's Wren‡ *Thryomanes bewickii* | r |  | r |  |
| House Wren *Troglodytes aedon* | c* | c | t |  |
| Winter Wren *Troglodytes troglodytes* | r* | r | u | u |
| Golden-crowned Kinglet *Regulus satrapa* | o |  | um | o |
| Ruby-crowned Kinglet *Regulus calendula* | um |  | um | t |
| Blue-gray Gnatcatcher *Polioptila caerulea* | um* | u | om |  |
| Eastern Bluebird *Sialia sialis* | o* | o | um | t |
| Townsend's Solitaire *Myadestes townsendi* |  |  | a |  |
| Veery *Catharus fuscescens* | om* | u | o |  |
| Gray-cheeked Thrush *Catharus minimus* | rm |  | rm |  |
| Swainson's Thrush *Catharus ustulatus* | om |  | om | t |
| Hermit Thrush *Catharus guttatus* | om* | o | u | t |
| Wood Thrush *Hylocichla mustelina* | c* | c | um |  |
| American Robin *Turdus migratorius* | c* | c | c | o |
| Gray Catbird *Dumetella carolinensis* | c* | c | o | r |
| Northern Mockingbird (P) *Mimus polyglottos* | c* | c | u | c |
| Brown Thrasher *Toxostoma rufum* | u* | u | o |  |
| Water Pipit *Anthus spinoletta* |  |  | rm |  |
| Bohemian Waxwing *Bombycilla garrulus* |  |  | rm |  |
| Cedar Waxwing *Bombycilla cedrorum* | o* | o | cm | u |
| Northern Shrike *Lanius excubitor* |  |  |  | t |
| European Starling *Sturnus vulgaris* | o* | o | t | t |
| White-eyed Vireo *Vireo griseus* | rm |  | rm |  |
| Solitary Vireo *Vireo solitarius* | um |  | um |  |
| Yellow-throated Vireo *Vireo flavifrons* | rm |  | om |  |
| Warbling Vireo *Vireo gilvus* | rm |  | rm |  |
| Philadelphia Vireo *Vireo philadelphicus* | rm |  | om |  |
| Red-eyed Vireo *Vireo olivaceus* | c* | c | om |  |
| Blue-winged Warbler *Vermivora pinus* | om* | u | om |  |
| "Brewster's" Warbler *Vermivora "leucobronchialis"* |  | r |  |  |
| Golden-winged Warbler *Vermivora chrysoptera* | r* | r |  |  |
| Tennessee Warbler *Vermivora peregrina* | om |  | om |  |
| Orange-crowned Warbler *Vermivora celata* | rm |  | rm |  |
| Nashville Warbler *Vermivora ruficapilla* | rm* | r | om |  |
| Northern Parula *Parula americana* | om | r | om |  |
| Yellow Warbler *Dendroica petechia* | c* | c | t |  |
| Chestnut-sided Warbler *Dendroica pensylvanica* | o* | o | om |  |
| Magnolia Warbler *Dendroica magnolia* | um | t | um |  |
| Cape May Warbler *Dendroica tigrina* | om |  | om |  |
| Black-throated Blue Warbler *Dendroica caerulescens* | om* | u | om |  |
| Yellow-rumped Warbler *Dendroica coronata* | um | t | cm | o |
| Black-throated Green Warbler *Dendroica virens* | r* | r | cm |  |
| Blackburnian Warbler *Dendroica fusca* | um |  | um |  |
| Yellow-throated Warbler *Dendroica dominica* | rm |  | rm |  |
| Pine Warbler *Dendroica pinus* | rm |  | rm |  |
| Prairie Warbler *Dendroica discolor* | o* |  | rm |  |
| Palm Warbler *Dendroica palmarum* | o |  | rm |  |
| Bay-breasted Warbler *Dendroica castanea* | um |  | um |  |
| Blackpoll Warbler *Dendroica striata* | um |  | um |  |
| Cerulean Warbler *Dendroica cerulea* | o* | o | um |  |
| Black-and-white Warbler *Mniotilta varia* | u* | u | um |  |
| American Redstart *Setophaga ruticilla* | u* | u | um |  |
| Prothonotary Warbler *Protonotaria citrea* | rm |  | rm |  |
| Worm-eating Warbler *Helmitheros vermivorus* | o* | o | rm |  |
| Ovenbird *Seiurus aurocapillus* | c* | c | um |  |
| Northern Waterthrush *Seiurus noveboracensis* | um |  | om |  |
| Louisiana Waterthrush *Seiurus motacilla* | o* | o | om |  |
| Kentucky Warbler *Oporornis formosus* | o* | o |  |  |
| Connecticut Warbler *Oporornis agilis* | rm |  | rm |  |
| Mourning Warbler *Oporornis philadelphia* | rm |  | rm |  |

| | Sp | S | F | W |
|---|---|---|---|---|
| Common Yellowthroat *Geothlypis trichas* | um* | c | um | |
| Hooded Warbler *Wilsonia citrina* | rm* | o | rm | |
| Wilson's Warbler *Wilsonia pusilla* | rm | t | rm | |
| Canada Warbler *Wilsonia canadensis* | r* | r | om | |
| Yellow-breasted Chat *Icteria virens* | r* | r | | |
| Summer Tanager *Piranga rubra* | | | rm | |
| Scarlet Tanager *Piranga olivacea* | c* | c | o | |
| Northern Cardinal (P) *Cardinalis cardinalis* | c* | c | c | c |
| Rose-breasted Grosbeak *Pheucticus ludovicianus* | c* | c | um | |
| Blue Grosbeak *Guiraca caerulea* | | a | rm | |
| Indigo Bunting *Passerina cyanea* | c* | c | t | |
| Dickcissel *Spiza americana* | | | r | |
| Rufous-sided Towhee *Pipilo erythrophthalmus* | c* | c | t | t |
| American Tree Sparrow *Spizella arborea* | o | | u | u |
| Chipping Sparrow *Spizella passerina* | c* | c | t | t |
| Field Sparrow *Spizella pusilla* | r* | r | t | |
| Vesper Sparrow *Pooecetes gramineus* | o | o | o | |
| Savannah Sparrow *Passerculus sandwichensis* | o | o | a | |
| Grasshopper Sparrow *Ammodramus savannarum* | o | r | | r |
| Henslow's Sparrow *Ammodramus henslowii* | a | | a | |
| Fox Sparrow *Passerella iliaca* | cm | | cm | t |
| Song Sparrow *Melospiza melodia* | u* | u | t | t |
| Lincoln's Sparrow *Melospiza lincolnii* | rm | | rm | |
| Swamp Sparrow *Melospiza georgiana* | o | | o | |
| White-throated Sparrow *Zonotrichia albicollis* | um | | um | c |
| White-crowned Sparrow *Zonotrichia leucophrys* | om | | um | |
| Dark-eyed Junco *Junco hyemalis* | u* | u | c | c |
| Lapland Longspur *Calcarius lapponicus* | | | a | |
| Snow Bunting *Plectrophenax nivalis* | | | om | t |
| Bobolink *Dolichonyx oryzivorus* | o | | rm | |
| Red-winged Blackbird *Agelaius phoeniceus* | c* | c | cm | |
| Eastern Meadowlark *Sturnella magna* | u* | u | om | |
| Yellow-headed Blackbird *Xanthocephalus xanthocephalus* | | | rm | |
| Rusty Blackbird *Euphagus carolinus* | rm | | om | t |
| Brewer's Blackbird *Euphagus cyanocephalus* | | | rm | |
| Common Grackle *Quiscalus quiscula* | cm | u | cm | |
| Brown-headed Cowbird *Molothrus ater* | c* | c | cm | t |
| Orchard Oriole *Icterus spurius* | r | | | |
| Northern Oriole *Icterus galbula* | c* | c | u | |
| Pine Grosbeak *Pinicola enucleator* | o | | o | t |
| Purple Finch *Carpodacus purpureus* | u* | r | u | u |
| House Finch (P) *Carpodacus mexicanus* | c* | c | c | c |
| Red Crossbill *Loxia curvirostra* | o | | o | t |
| White-winged Crossbill *Loxia leucoptera* | a | | o | t |
| Common Redpoll *Carduelis flammea* | o | | o | t |
| Hoary Redpoll *Carduelis hornemanni* | a | | | t |
| Pine Siskin *Carduelis pinus* | u | t | u | u |
| American Goldfinch (P) *Carduelis pinus* | c | c* | c | c |
| Evening Grosbeak *Coccothraustes vespertinus* | u | | u | u |
| House Sparrow *Passer domesticus* | u* | u | u | u |

Sp = spring (March–May).
S  = summer (June–August).
F  = fall (September–November).
W = winter (December–February).
(P) = permanent resident at Hawk Mountain.
m = migrant; seen or heard during spring or fall migration.
c  = commonly seen or heard during season.
u  = uncommon; seen or heard during season in variable numbers.
o  = occasionally seen or heard a few times during season.
r  = rare; previously noted, but rarely seen or heard.
t  = transient; temporary visitor or straggler during season.
a  = accidental; one record during season.
*  = breeding or has bred.
　　†Whip-poor-wills were regular breeders on the sanctuary up until the late sixties.
　　‡Bewick's wrens were last recorded in 1951.
　　Nomenclature from American Ornithologists' Union, *Check-list of North American Birds*, 6th ed. (Washington, D.C.: AOU, 1983).

# Suggested Reading

Brooks, Maurice. *The Appalachians*. Boston: Houghton Mifflin, 1965.

Broun, Maurice. *Hawks Aloft: The Story of Hawk Mountain*. 50th anniversary edition. Kempton, Penn.: Hawk Mountain Sanctuary Assoc. by arrangement with Dodd, Mead, New York, 1984. Originally published by Dodd, Mead, 1948.

Brown, Leslie, and Dean Amadon. *Eagles, Hawks, and Falcons of the World*. 2 vols. New York: McGraw-Hill, 1948, reissued 1968.

Brunner, D. B. *The Indians of Berks County, Pennsylvania, being a Summary of all the Tangible Records of the Aborigines of Berks County*. Reading, Penn.: Eagle Book Print, 1891. Available in the rare book sections of the Kutztown University Library, Kutztown, Penn., and the Reading Public Library, Reading, Penn.

Clark, William S., and Brian K. Wheeler. *Hawks*. Peterson Field Guide no. 35. Boston: Houghton Mifflin, 1987.

Dunne, Peter, Debbie Keller, and Rene Kochenberger. *Hawk Watch: A Guide for Beginners*. Cape May, N.J.: Cape May Bird Observatory/ New Jersey Audubon Society, 1984.

Dunne, Peter, David Sibley, and Clay Sutton. *Hawks in Flight*. Boston: Houghton Mifflin, 1988.

Harwood, Michael. *The View from Hawk Mountain*. New York: Scribner, 1973.

———, ed. *Hawk Mountain News: 50th Anniversary Edition*. No. 62. September 1984.

Heintzelman, Donald S. *Autumn Hawk Flights: The Migrations in Eastern North America*. New Brunswick, N.J.: Rutgers University Press, 1975.

———. *A Guide to Eastern Hawk Watching*. University Park: Pennsylvania State University Press, 1976.

McPhee, John. *In Suspect Terrain*. New York: Farrar, Straus & Giroux, 1983. A geologic history of the northeastern Appalachian Mountains.

Shelford, Victor. *The Ecology of North America*. Urbana: University of Illinois Press, 1963.

Shepps, Vincent C. *Pennsylvania and the Ice Age*. Pennsylvania Topographic and Geologic Service Education Series, no. 6. Harrisburg: Pennsylvania Dept. of Environmental Resources, 1962.

Wherry, Edgar T., John M. Fogg, Jr., and Herbert A. Wahl. *Atlas of the Flora of Pennsylvania*. Philadelphia: The Morris Arboretum of the University of Pennsylvania, 1979.

Wilhusen, J. P. *Geology of the Appalachian Trail in Pennsylvania*. Pennsylvania Geological Survey Series, no. 4. Harrisburg: Pennsylvania Dept. of Environmental Resources, 1983.

# Index

Numbers in italic type refer to pages with illustrations.

**113**